THE WRIGHT STYLE

CARLA LIND

AN ARCHETYPE PRESS BOOK

SIMON & SCHUSTER

NEW YORK LONDON TORONTO SYDNEY TOKYO

SIMON & SCHUSTER
Simon & Schuster Building
Rockefeller Center
1230 Avenue of the Americas
New York, New York 10020

SIMON & SCHUSTER and its colophon are registered trademarks of Simon & Schuster Inc.

Library of Congress Cataloging-in-Publication Data
Lind, Carla
The Wright style / Carla Lind.
     p.   cm.
"An Archetype Press book."
Includes bibliographical references and index.
ISBN 0-671-74959-5 : $40.00
1. Dwellings—United States—Themes, motives. 2. Wright, Frank
Lloyd, 1867–1959—Criticism and interpretation. I. Title.
NA7205.L56 1992
728'. 37'092—dc20   91-44553

Printed and bound in Hong Kong
10 9 8 7

Endpapers courtesy Schumacher

Quotation sources: page 20. *House Beautiful,* November 1955. Hearst
Corporation. page 23. *Frank Lloyd Wright: His Living Voice.* The Press
at California State University. © 1987 Frank Lloyd Wright Foundation.
pages 28–31. *In the Cause of Architecture: Frank Lloyd Wright.*
An Architectural Record Book. © 1975 McGraw-Hill, Inc. page 64.
An Autobiography. Frank Lloyd Wright. Duell, Sloan and Pearce, 1943.
© 1932, 1943, 1977 Frank Lloyd Wright Foundation. page 99. *Frank
Lloyd Wright's Fallingwater: The House and Its History.* Donald Hoffmann.
© 1978 Dover Publications, Inc. pages 113, 120. *The Pope-Leighey House.*
Terry B. Morton, ed. National Trust for Historic Preservation, 1969.
page 165. *R. M. Schindler House, 1921–1922.* Produced for Friends
of the Schindler House. Perpetua Press. ©1987 Kathryn Smith.

Photograph, page 1: The entrance gate Frank Lloyd Wright designed for the Lovness studio in Stillwater, Minnesota, picks up geometric designs in the house itself. Wright's favorite color, Cherokee red, was chosen for the gate's iron pipe. [Domino's Center for Architecture and Design]

Photograph, pages 4–5: Wright's organic architecture seamlessly blended outside and in, carefully framing views of nature. The living room window of his home Taliesin captures his beloved Wisconsin countryside. An art glass design from the Heath house in Buffalo, New York, is set into the window. [© Yukio Futagawa]

Photograph, pages 2–3: Fallingwater, Wright's famous house cantilevered over a waterfall, melds house and site like few other buildings have ever done. The stone and concrete masterpiece rises from the rocky bed of a mountain stream near Mill Run, Pennsylvania, and is embraced by abundant vegetation on the hillside. [Christopher Little]

Photograph, pages 6–7: The barrel-vaulted children's playroom in Wright's own Oak Park home shows how the young architect was able to expand space visually even early in his career. The pureness of the geometric forms and the decorative elements in the room reflect Wright's training with Froebel blocks when he was a boy. [Jon Miller, © Hedrich-Blessing]

Produced by Archetype Press, Inc., Washington, D.C.

Project Director: Diane Maddex
Art Director: Robert L. Wiser

Production Assistants: Melton Castro, Derrick Johnson, Marc Meadows, and Nancy Spangler

Opposite: Wright's Dana-Thomas house in Springfield, Illinois, completed in 1904, is a symphony of autumn colors, geometric designs, and dramatic spaces. The magical art glass window patterns are derived from natural forms, most notably the angular shapes of sumac leaves. [© Judith Bromley]

INTRODUCTION

Frank Lloyd Wright was America's very own architect. He was a
product of the country's pioneer, can-do spirit who revolutionized
the way Americans thought about their buildings and towns. Drawing
inspiration from his native midwestern prairie, he coaxed Americans
out of their boxlike houses and into wide-open living spaces that
suited the American lifestyle. He rejected the classical designs
borrowed from other worlds that so dominated the architecture of
the late nineteenth and early twentieth centuries. Instead, he gave
America a blueprint for its own architecture, one based on simplicity
and the lessons of nature. He called it organic architecture.

His career spanned seven decades and two centuries.
From 1885 until his death in 1959, he received more than a thousand
commissions, nearly half of which resulted in completed structures.
Six out of every seven of these still stand. Wright remains the most
prolific architect America has ever known. His buildings are scattered
from coast to coast, in thirty-six states and three foreign countries.
Nestled into woods, projecting from mountaintops, stretched over
suburban acres, sculpted from hillsides, defining city blocks, or
blending with the desert floor, nearly every building is a unique
response to the client and the site for which it was designed. Equally
diverse are their functions. The versatility of Wright's talent resulted
in masterpieces for living, working, worshiping, learning, performing,
and even a plan for an entire city. Their beauty stems from the
essence, the very nature, of each individual project. The architecture
was not imposed on the building's purpose but was a response to it.

Wright's greatest contribution was his fresh look at residential architecture, the focus of this book. Throughout his career, he
was obsessed with defining the perfect living space for contemporary
life. In fact, an overwhelming majority of his commissions—eighty
percent of his more than four hundred surviving buildings—are residences or their outbuildings. He carefully studied society, its innova-
tions, its absurdities, and its relationship with the natural world. He
saw an America that was informal, independent, asymmetrical. Yet it
was housed in confined, formal, symmetrical boxes that were
adorned with elements drawn from European history. He sought to
give America its own architectural identity that fit its people, land-
scapes, and technologies. And what an impact he had.

Wright's ideas have so permeated our architectural world
that we have lost track of the source. His open floor plans led to

family rooms, kitchens open to living areas, indoor spaces open to outdoor living spaces, garden rooms, decks, and carports. His use of glass opened window walls and brought generous amounts of light and inspiring vistas into rooms. He altered America's collective subconscious. By bringing together many elements and inspirations, most neither new nor original, he was able to synthesize fresh new forms that reflected the character of the nation.

His productivity appears even greater when each commission is analyzed. Every one of the more than three hundred residences he designed was a complex composition of numerous interrelated elements. He created not merely the shell of a building but its decorative arts as well. The art glass windows and skylights, furniture, light fixtures, textiles, carpets, fireplace andirons, wall murals, wall finishes, any integral ornament, and landscaping all were part of the unified design he envisioned for a client. This approach resulted in thousands of individual designs. Fortunately, he was always surrounded by devoted apprentices and artisans who could interpret and execute his design ideology in its many manifestations. Although he tried, it was humanly impossible for one person to follow through on each detail of every job. By necessity, his apprentices became ambassadors—extra hands—enabling Wright's genius to have an even deeper and broader impact.

Wright's need to communicate his revolutionary vision was insatiable. But so is the public's hunger for his ideas. Those who came in contact with him, whether in an audience, on a street, or in his office, were left with an indelible memory that they would speak of for years to come. Periodic surveys still rate him as America's greatest architect, despite the fact that he has been dead for more than thirty years.

His words, as well as the beauty of his designs, have gradually sensitized more and more American families so that when they look for a home or discuss plans with an architect, they have the courage to express what they want and need, expecting a sensitive, meaningful response. He brought architecture to the people. Wright made us feel that good residential architecture was within our reach.

Contrasts that appealed to Wright can be seen at Fallingwater, where at night light plays against dark, glass against stone, horizontal against vertical, elegance against simplicity. [Christopher Little]

THE WRIGHT STYLE

FRANK LLOYD WRIGHT'S ARCHITECTURE WAS ROOTED IN NATURE; HE CALLED IT ORGANIC. AT THE HEART OF HIS WORK WAS SIMPLICITY, HARMONY, UNITY, AND INTEGRITY. HE TOSSED OUT OUR BOXLIKE SPACES, FOREVER CHANGING THE IDEA OF WHAT A HOUSE COULD BE.

Previous pages: Nature was Wright's greatest teacher. His lessons were rooted in the essence of natural forms, rhythms, colors, and structures. The roots of a tree, the palette of the season, and the filtered light of Wisconsin woods became an inspirational textbook for his organic designs. [Michael J. Shedlock]

Opposite: The dining room Wright created for his Oak Park home in 1895 exemplifies the unity he achieved even in his earliest work. He reached beyond the design of the house itself to all of the elements in the room. Wright took control of the entire space by designing the furniture, including the high chair; the recessed

lighting, which was filtered through a wooden grille; and the cabinets, crafted to conceal the radiators. The result was a total, unified environment, one of the first of many he strove to create in his seventy-year career. [Jon Miller, © Hedrich-Blessing]

ORIGINS

There is a certain irony in talking about a "Wright style," because the uniformity this term implies probably would be viewed negatively by Wright himself. To Wright, the inherent differences in each building, designed to fit the needs of each client and the attributes of each site, defied grouping it into a category. The only "style" involved was how well a building was designed to serve its own purpose. Wright suggested that "as humanity develops, there will be less recourse to the 'styles' and more style . . . that quality in each that was once painfully achieved by the whole." His own work clearly reflected this attitude. Each Wright-designed structure was unique and vital. That was *his* style. Yet there is an undeniable commonality about the vast number of designs that burst forth from this artistic genius.

Frank Lloyd Wright's creations were based on a life philosophy that was undeniably rooted in his childhood. Further shaped by his life experiences, his designs developed distinct attributes that, when repeated, pushed some of his buildings helplessly into sub-styles such as Prairie (1901–1913), textile block (1917–1924), and Usonian (1936–1959), terms used by Wright himself. While useful, these terms do not do justice to the individuality of each building, and they do not describe many of his designs that cannot be neatly labeled. Like any great artist, his work has been grouped into periods to denote shifts in his personal and professional direction. Such categories, like his buildings, are not boxes; instead, they are open and informal shelters. Wright called the totality of his work organic architecture. This concept provides the breadth and flexibility required to define Wright's style as he and his followers have practiced it for the past century. It is far more enduring than the term "style" implies.

To Wright, standardization was useful but should not limit the architect's vision. In fact, his fascination with technology and his desire to bring good design into the homes of average Americans led to several production-line projects, for prefabricated houses, glass-ware, fabrics, wallpapers, and furniture. By agreeing to design lines of interior furnishings, he was certainly selling his "style," because for the most part they would not be used in buildings he designed.

Many fibers in Wright's life were woven together to create a unified, ideological tapestry just as all of the elements in his buildings were combined and interrelated to yield a complete composition for living. Wright acknowledged that some of the fibers contributed more to the ultimate fabric than others.

UNITY

The origins of Frank Lloyd Wright's aesthetic sensitivity can be traced to his youth. His mother, Anna Lloyd Wright, the child of tough, Unitarian, Welsh farmers, introduced her son to many of the experiences that shaped his life. Anna Lloyd-Jones was raised in the Wisconsin River Valley near Spring Green, Wisconsin, and she loved the earth. Wright described her as being "in league with the stones of the field." Anna had a vision for her son—that he would become a great architect. Thus, his early education, at home and at school, was directed toward this goal. She provided a simple but stimulating environment for his learning. Her maternal influence was augmented by the dominating Lloyd-Jones family. Wright frequently visited the Wisconsin farms of his uncles and learned firsthand about hard work, simplicity, and self-confidence.

The concept of unity was a compelling early lesson. So intrinsic was it to the Unitarianism of his family that it must have played an indelible role in creating his world view. As he recalled in his autobiography, "Unity was their watchword, the sign and symbol that thrilled them, the Unity of all things!" Wright's grandfather, father, and uncles were powerful preachers who pounded the concepts of their faith into the depths of the soul of the child. Unity—a oneness with the world, with God, with all forms of life. Truth, truth above all, truth against the world, the beauty of truth. This refrain also echoed in Wright's young world. How could these concepts be forgotten as he forged his own philosophy? They could not. They became its foundation.

Left: Wright felt especially at home in the Wisconsin countryside. Here he surveys the view outside Taliesin about 1928. [Frank Lloyd Wright Archives]

Opposite above: The Wrights enjoyed an active family life. Just a year after their marriage in 1889, Wright (seated at right) and his relatives gathered on the front steps of his Oak Park home. With him, from left, are Jenkin Lloyd-Jones, an uncle; Susan Lloyd-Jones, an aunt; his sister Jane; his wife, Catherine, with baby Lloyd; Anna Lloyd Wright, his mother; Maginel, a sister; and Mary, a cousin. [Frank Lloyd Wright Home and Studio Foundation]

Opposite bottom: Wright also found quiet moments to read and take this self-portrait on the terrace in Oak Park. He saw his home as a refuge and a stimulating gathering place. [Frank Lloyd Wright Archives]

MUSIC

Wright's father made a lasting impact on the architect's aesthetics, although some historians have considered him, unlike Wright's mother, an insignificant and somewhat temporary influence. Like the Lloyd-Jones family, William Russell Cary Wright also was a Unitarian, a minister as well as a lawyer and musician. From him, Wright discovered his passion for Baroque music. As a child, he would lay awake listening to his father playing Beethoven on the piano. The interplay of the notes, the minor themes and major themes, the harmony, the building, the movement from general to particulars, all deeply affected the way he viewed his world. Music did not merely entertain him but also enriched his life in many ways. It provided an analogous system that he could use to help translate his ideas into another art form, architecture. In his autobiography, Wright described the commonalities between an architect and a musician: "the striving for entity, oneness in diversity, depth in design, repose in the final expression of the whole. I am going to a delightful inspiring school when I listen to Beethoven's music."

In a special edition of *House Beautiful* magazine published in 1955, Wright, then eighty-eight, wrote:

What I call integral ornament is founded upon the same organic simplicities as Beethoven's Fifth Symphony, that amazing revolution in tumult and splendor of sound built upon four tones, based upon a rhythm a child could play on the piano with one finger. Supreme imagination reared the four repeated tones, simple rhythms, into a great symphonic poem that is probably the noblest thought-built edifice in our world. And architecture is like music in this capacity for the symphony.

To Wright, both music and architecture were sublimated mathematics. He credited his father with making the comparison by referring to a symphony as an "edifice of sound."

Music was always an integral part of Wright's life at Taliesin. When he was there he made time to play the piano, a skill his father taught him at an early age. Music gave Wright relaxation and inspiration. In the masterworks of Bach and Beethoven he found analogies to architecture. [Ezra Stoller, © Esto]

Right: Nature inspired Wright in many ways. Concrete sprites at Taliesin West recall the patterns of desert cactus. [Richard Bowditch]

Below: Limestone outcroppings were translated into naturally laid stone walls at Taliesin. [Balthazar Korab] Yucca flowers, in the hands of Wright student Gene Masselink, became an abstract geometric pattern. [Tony Puttnam, Frank Lloyd Wright Foundation]

Opposite: Wright borrowed the angular forms of mountains for the rubble walls of Taliesin West. A sumac plant was abstracted to create art glass for the Dana-Thomas house. [Tony Puttnam, Frank Lloyd Wright Foundation]

NATURE

Nature, above all else, was Wright's most inspirational force. He advised his students to "study nature, love nature, stay close to nature. It will never fail you." His childhood experiences on the family homesteads in the rugged, driftless area of southwestern Wisconsin put him in touch with the rhythms, patterns, colors, and systems of nature. The simple concept of the interdependence of all living things was absorbed at an early age. Nature was synonymous with God to Wright, and it was his greatest teacher. Through his mother, Wright also learned to appreciate the work of the naturalist writers of the time: Whittier, Lowell, Emerson, Blake, and Thoreau. Their writings encouraged him to find wisdom in the natural world.

In 1953, in one of his Sunday morning spontaneous talks to his students, Wright advised them:

The place for an architect to study construction first of all, before he gets into the theory of the various formulas that exist in connection with steel beams, girders, and reinforced concrete, is the study of Nature. In Nature you will find everything exemplified, from the blade of grass to the tree, from the tree to the geological formations to the procession of the eras beginning with the first from the sea downwards. . . .

That doesn't mean you are to go out and just look at the hills and the ways the animals conduct themselves. . . . The study of Nature, Nature with a capital N, Nature, inner Nature, Nature of the hand, of this apparatus, of this glass. The truth concerning all those things is architectural study.

He did not suggest copying nature but, instead, allowing it to be an inspiration, understanding the fundamental principles and elements—its essence. The visual delights that nature provides became a part of his designs as well. The sympathetic relationship between site and building, the easy transitions from the inside to the outside, the gardens and planters all illustrate a respect for the natural world that is compelling. It is difficult to visit one of Wright's buildings and not interact, in a memorable way, with its setting. He built homes around trees, rather than remove them. He used the sun's power to help warm the rooms and provide an ever-changing pattern of light and shadow. He framed views, both nearby and distant. He borrowed nature's devices to provide repose using the line of the horizon, to extend reach using the cantilever like a branch, to create protective shelter like a natural cave. The interplay of people, building, and site was harmonious and masterful.

GEOMETRY

As a result of Anna Lloyd Wright's continuous search for educational techniques that would encourage young Frank's creative skills, she discovered the Froebel blocks. These teaching tools for Friedrich Froebel's kindergarten education program introduced Wright to geometry, spatial relationships, and systems in a fundamental way. The program's basic theme was that child's play could be gently guided, using specific techniques, toward a greater appreciation for the elements and laws of nature. The tools were simple, pure shapes, unlike the gawdy, frivolous toys of the period.

It is from the Froebel "gifts," as they were called, that he learned the basic forms of nature—geometric forms—in two and three dimensions. First, he worked with colored yarn shapes, then smooth maple blocks in cubes, spheres, and triangles, then colorful cardboard shapes made into patterns on a tabletop grid. Each exercise was a new problem that challenged the budding designer. As a child, he spent hours with these gifts, later attributing to them a formative and lasting influence on his architecture. Their impact was apparent in every building Wright ever designed.

From nature and elemental geometry grew Wright's ability to abstract natural forms—reducing a flower or leaf to pure geometric shapes. This pattern could then be manipulated in various combinations into a new composition. These geometric exercises became the sources of floor plans, elevations, and decorative arts, each element generated from the same design theme. Once converted into three-dimensional forms, the elements would all work together in harmony like the natural shapes that were their source. Each building was given its own lexicon of forms, a language then used throughout the design. The art glass related to the furniture, which related to the moldings, which related to the floor plan, which related to the site plan. They became inextricably linked through geometry.

Abstracted natural motifs were used for art glass window designs in the early houses. Sometimes, a specific plant was selected, such as the tulip in the 1895 playroom of his own home in Oak Park or the sumac in the Dana-Thomas house of 1904. But in other commissions, such as the May house of 1908 in Grand Rapids, Michigan, a more generic plant form appears to be the source.

A thematic, geometric design was cast into the concrete blocks that Wright first introduced in California about 1920. In the Freeman house alone are fifty-two versions of the block design, which apparently is based on an abstraction of the site plan with a grove of eucalyptus. The variations of this basic design were repeated over and over and when massed into walls create a pattern and rhythm of their own.

In 1936 Wright designed his first Usonian house, a word he used to describe buildings uniquely suitable for life in the United States. In these houses, the abstractions are even clearer than in his early Prairie Style designs. Each home was based on a geometric grid used both in plan and in elevation. The two-by-four-foot rectangular module of the first Jacobs residence in Madison, Wisconsin, was drawn on the architectural plans as well as scored into the concrete floor. The module, or unit of design, selected for a particular building would twist and turn and be repeated over and over in the floor plan and elevations. Squares, hexagons, circles, parallelograms, and triangles also were used at different times as the basis for building designs.

Opposite: The May house windows are typical of the simply divided panels Wright used to complement natural forms outside while repeating a house's architectural forms. Wheatlike clusters rise from rectangular piers, flanked by horizontal ledge shapes. A set of Froebel blocks underneath this window shows one of Wright's formative architectural inspirations from childhood. "I sat at the little kindergarten tabletop," he later reflected, "and played...with the cube, the sphere, and the triangle. I learned to see this way and when I did, I did not care to draw casual incidentals of Nature. I wanted to design." [John Boucher, Steelcase]

Opposite: Wright learned about integral ornament from his early employer, Louis Sullivan. Wright, however, applied a more geometrical structure to his designs such as the bronze-green, plaster frieze that surrounds the Dana-Thomas house in Springfield, Illinois. The sumac plant, used elsewhere in the house, was abstracted here to become the design's central figure.

Below: At a time when Victorian, excessively ornate houses dominated the domestic scene, Wright looked to simplicity as more meaningful and visually rewarding. He found inspiration in Japanese architecture, which may have influenced his use of sheltering, low-pitched, upturned roofs in the Dana-Thomas house. [Photographs © Judith Bromley]

LOUIS SULLIVAN

Wright moved to Chicago from his native Wisconsin in 1887, leaving the University of Wisconsin after only two semesters. He first apprenticed with Joseph Lyman Silsbee, who was actively introducing the Shingle Style to the Midwest. Within a year, Wright began his tenure at the side of Louis Sullivan, whom he would thereafter refer to as his *lieber Meister* (beloved master). Sullivan also inspired Wright to look at nature's rhythms and processes and to create architecture that related to contemporary life. Sullivan, the philosophical father of what became known as the Prairie School, provided the rhetoric that called for an American architecture that was not bound by tradition. More practically, he taught Wright about ornament. Rather than applied, he believed, it should be integral to the building itself. Wright learned from Sullivan that the elements of a building could provide all of the ornamentation that was needed. Again the refrain that governed Wright's work—simplicity, unity, nature.

JAPANESE DESIGN

Wright also was profoundly influenced by Japanese design. His first exposure was the imperial Japanese exhibit at the World's Columbian Exposition in Chicago in 1893. Known as the Ho-ho-den, its fluid spaces were covered by a broad, sheltering roof, with generous overhanging eaves. Light poured in from all sides. The walls moved, opening up spaces, releasing the box. This experience provided more data for Wright's creative mind to devour and synthesize.

The simplicity of Japanese design also revealed itself in Japanese wood-block prints, which combined his love of nature and the pureness of geometry. His fascination with them began as a young man. When he and his first wife, Catherine, visited Japan for the first time in 1905, he was able to study Japanese architecture and roam the back alleys in search of prints. At various times in his life, his impressive collection of Japanese art was sold to pay debts, and at other periods it grew to include screens, kimonos, ceramics, and textiles. But the print remained as a symbol of simplicity and elimination of all that was unnecessary. This quality provided such a pivotal impact on his design aesthetic that he published his first book, *The Japanese Print*, on the subject in 1910.

ORGANIC ARCHITECTURE

Through years of careful, intuitive observation, study, and experimentation, Wright was able to translate his unique concept of architecture into a total design ideology that he called organic architecture. He welcomed opportunities to articulate this ideology in lectures and publications throughout his life. Perhaps the act of organizing his thoughts and communicating them so frequently helped instill them so securely in his own behavior that the architectural consistency was sure to follow—it may have been the synthesizing process that pulled it all together. His work embodied his ideals. He truly created a new architectural language.

In 1894, at age twenty-seven, he is thought to have conceived a famous essay, "In the Cause of Architecture," that was ultimately published in *The Architectural Record* in 1908. In the essay, he set forth propositions that established an enduring grammar for his work and that of his followers. Here is a summary of this advice, which included some very specific suggestions:

☐ "Simplicity and repose are the qualities that measure the true value of any work of art." Limit the number of rooms and spaces to only what is needed. Openings should be seen as part of the structure. Eliminate unnecessary detail and ornament (for example, use a piece of wood without an extra molding, a plain wooden slat rather than a turned baluster, plain fabrics and floor coverings). Build in unsightly appliances and equipment. Use pictures only as part of an overall scheme. Build in as much furniture as possible. Consider the whole as an integral unit. Use simple unbroken wall surfaces from the water table to the roof (or the frieze below the roof).

☐ Each home should express the owners' individuality and be unique.

The Robie house of 1908 in Chicago's Hyde Park neighborhood is a masterful example of Wright's concept of organic architecture. The low hipped roof, broad overhangs, Roman brick courses, and limestone planters and copings create layers of horizontal lines that accent bold masonry masses. [Balthazar Korab]

☐ A building should appear to grow easily from its site. Design gently sloping roofs (low-pitch hipped, unbroken; low with pediments on long ridges; or a simple slab). Keep proportions low. Use suppressed heavy chimneys. Build sheltering overhangs. Include low terraces. Construct garden walls that reach out.

☐ Use natural colors. "Go to the woods and fields for color schemes." Choose warm, soft tones of earth and autumn. Do not select pessimistic blues, purples, or cool colors of the "ribbon counter."

☐ Bring out the nature of materials. Use natural wood finishes. Show the natural texture of plaster with stain applied to it. Reveal the friendly and beautiful nature of all materials.

☐ Put the machine to work to serve civilization. Maximize its usefulness (for example, use furniture with clean-cut, straight-line forms).

☐ Eliminate the boxlike compartments we live in. Open up the spaces.

☐ Group windows in a rhythmic way. Use casement windows, not double-hung, guillotine-style windows.

☐ Create floor plans in an axial and balanced order. Conceive room designs in three dimensions.

☐ Provide a place for natural foliage or flowers. Use urns, planters, garden walls.

☐ Use ornamentation that is of the building. Ornament is "constitutional" and begins with the building's conception. Create art glass windows with straight-line patterns that suit the characteristics of the glass and metal components.

☐ Determine one form for a particular building and adhere to that motif throughout the building, designing every detail of the whole.

☐ As it grows older, a house with character will grow more valuable than one that is merely in "fashion."

☐ Above all, strive for integrity.

These concepts were the fundamentals of Wright's style. Certainly, they were the marks of his Prairie Style houses, designed from the turn of the twentieth century to the mid-teens. For six decades, Wright articulated these same principles in varying ways, but he never deviated from them. In May 1952 he defined the terms of organic architecture for *Architectural Record* once again. He reiterated his principles, but this time the specifics related more to his Usonian houses than to their Prairie Style predecessors.

Organic architecture was definitely a new sense of shelter for *humane* life. Shelter, broad and low. Roofs, either flat or pitched, hipped or gabled, but always comprehensive Shelter. Wide flat eaves were sometimes perforated to let trellised light through upon characteristic ranges of windows below. Ornament was nonexistent unless integral. Walls became screens, often glass screens, and the new open-plan spread space upon a concrete ground mat: the whole structure intimate and wide upon and of the ground itself. This ground-mat floor eventually contained the gravity-heating system (heat rises naturally as water falls) of the spaces to be lived in: forced circulation of hot water in pipes embedded in a broken stone bed beneath the floor slabs (soon misnamed "radiant heat"). Other new techniques, new forms adapted to our inevitable machine-methods appeared in these new structures. The economics of continuity and cantilevered structure were realized. Even the walls played a new role or disappeared altogether. A new sense of space in appropriate human scale pervaded not only the structure but the life itself lived in it was broadened, made more free because of sympathetic freedom of plan and structure. The interior space to be lived in became *the reality of the whole performance.* Building as a box, was gone. The integral character of the third dimension was born to architecture.

How did Wright's philosophy translate into actual buildings? What are the unique attributes that have become so identified with him? The following sections provide an overview of the elements that define his work. At the root of each was simplicity, and from simplicity came the harmony, unity, and integrity that we today identify as Wright's own style.

To break open boxlike spaces, Wright sought ways to dissolve corners. A mitered window in the Palmer garden house in Ann Arbor, Michigan, frees the interior space so that it becomes one with the outside. This Japanese-inspired teahouse actually was designed in 1964, after Wright's death, by his apprentice John Howe. Repeating Wright's module for the house itself, this intimate structure stands as a protective shelter yet welcomes the beauty of the garden—a harmonious landscape that grew from the teahouse. In their additions, both Howe and the Palmers have perpetuated Wright's principles of organic architecture. [© Judith Bromley]

Opposite: In the May house in Grand Rapids, Michigan, Wright created a perfectly unified, harmonious composition. Entering the home, one is compressed into a hallway, then released and drawn into the openness of the living area, moving freely from one space to another. [Jon Miller, © Hedrich-Blessing. Courtesy Steelcase]

Above: The 1948 Walker house on the beach at Carmel, California, reaches out like a ship's prow—at one with its site. [Balthazar Korab]

Below: To achieve a more human scale in the Martin house in Buffalo, New York, Wright used different ceiling heights and horizontal banding. [K. C. Kratt]

THE SITE

A Wright building and its site are wedded—one cannot be considered without the other. The most committed marriage of house to site is Fallingwater near Mill Run, Pennsylvania; cantilevered over a waterfall, the house is one with the rocky terrain. Similarly, the topography, the flora and fauna, and the other natural attributes of a location as well as the characteristics of the region influenced the appearance of Wright's other buildings. Houses built on the prairie, for example, reflected the whole area's horizontality, not just aspects of the specific site. In Wright's opinion, the horizontal line was the line of repose, tranquility, and domesticity. Each building, he proclaimed, should be *of* the earth, not perched *on* it.

SPACE

"The room within is the great fact about the building," wrote Wright in 1928. This space, the reason for the building itself, dictates the exterior shape. To Wright, spaces were meant to be fluid, free flowing, and informal like the American lifestyle. In Wright houses, living spaces tend to blend together. Closed rooms are limited to bathrooms and bedrooms. He beckoned Americans to break out of their boxes, reach outside—visually, through window walls, and actually, using terraces, porches, and sensitive site planning. He also used space as a technique for controlling experiences within a building. Entrances and rooms were often narrow and confining so that the space at the end would feel more expansive. Confine-and-release proved an effective exercise in contrasts, one that provokes a subliminal awe in those who experience Wright's spaces firsthand.

SCALE

The logical source of scale in his residences was, of course, the humans who inhabited them. More often than not, however, the scale he used was his own, five feet, eight inches. The structure's proposed use and building materials also contributed to the scale chosen, but once a unit of measure was determined it became the standard for the entire building and from it grew the proportions. Doorways and ceiling heights were brought down to a more human scale, creating a feeling of comfort and oneness with the architecture.

MATERIALS

Natural materials in their natural condition and place provided inspiration for Wright's buildings. To be most effective, the number of materials was limited. Once again, simplicity. One material was always primary, while others were merely supplementary. Exterior and interior materials were often the same, just as the exterior was an expression of the interior space. Wright explored the very essence and capabilities of each type of building material so it could be most expressive in his final design. The texture inherent in the dominant material provided a "feeling," an identity. The context of a building certainly played an important role in what was chosen. City and suburban dwellings were more likely to be built of even, level, brick; asymmetrical stone was more appropriate for the countryside.

☐ Stone. Of all the materials Wright used, he probably spoke about stone the most. He had great appreciation for this ancient building material and built Taliesin, his own home in Spring Green, Wisconsin, from native limestone carried from a nearby quarry and Taliesin West from the boulders found on the Arizona desert floor.

He looked to the quarry itself for guidance on how to lay up stone. "The rock ledges of a stone-quarry are a story and a longing to me. There is a suggestion in the strata and character in the formations," he wrote in 1928. A local stonemason who worked for Wright at Taliesin for fourteen years stated it in a different way: "Frank liked that stick-out stuff," he said, referring to the alternate layers of projecting stones with barely visible mortar that mimicked the quarry strata. For nearly fifty years, Wright continued to shape, mold, expand, and define Taliesin using stone. The apprentices who studied with him learned about its properties by building walls there. Local indigenous stone was specified for numerous commissions in

different areas of the country. The results were houses clearly in sympathy with their setting.

☐ Brick. Brick in a variety of colors, finishes, and dimensions was specified throughout Wright's career and was not limited to use as an exterior building material. He saw no need to hide what many regarded as too crude a material for the living room. He not only left it exposed inside but liberally used it to define the central core of his buildings. Whether he used brick of standard proportions or the flatter, Roman style, Wright often accented the horizontality of a building by requesting custom tooling and coloring of the mortar. Vertical joints were cut flush with the brick face and colored to match the brick, but horizontal joints were deeply raked to create a long shadow. A massive masonry chimney stood at the core of the majority of his residences and served as the focal point for family life as well as the design itself.

☐ Wood. Before advances in steel fabrication technology, Wright depended primarily on wood as his principal structural element. Those currently restoring his early homes are amazed at the confidence he had in the material. Its properties were certainly stretched as his bold new designs sometimes outpaced technology. But machine technologies were put to use to cut costs and enhance the qualities of wood. Using veneers helped reduce the ecological impact on forests and saved money.

For interiors, Wright favored certain woods during different periods of his career, but they were always used with great respect for their inherent beauty. He abhorred covering the intricate, luscious patterns of wood grain with paint or concealing its linear power with

Opposite: Wright combined his favorite materials at the entrance to his Oak Park studio. Common brick dominates the design but is richly accented with limestone, wood, shingles, glass, plaster ornament, and even nature's own flowers. Despite the variety of materials, simplicity prevails. [Jon Miller, © Hedrich-Blessing]

curvaceous turning or scrollwork. Stains and shellacs were sometimes used to enhance the color of the wood, and waxes and oils were preferred over varnishes. In the early years, oak, particularly quartersawn, was dominant, although he also used other woods such as birch, walnut, and maple. Later, cypress and Philippine mahogany were used extensively. A few of the early residences and numerous Usonian houses used broad boards and battens, often of cypress, as the principal building material both inside and out. The introduction of plywood offered new possibilities, because it, too, was inexpensive, durable, and flexible.

Simple bands of wood trim, sometimes called marking strips, inside and out defined surface planes and led the eye. This technique accented the horizontality and fluidity of the open spaces Wright created, which in turn helped relate a building's scale to the inhabitants.

☐ Plaster. Plaster finishes typically had a sand float and were sometimes stained or colored, rather than painted. Wright also used special painting techniques called stippling and scumbling to further enhance wall textures; these somewhat mottled finishes tended to dissolve the solidity of the wall, giving the illusion of more openness. Additionally, he cast plaster in molds with elaborate Sullivanesque patterns and integrated these panels into several of his early buildings, designs that frequently were mistaken for terra cotta. The stork panels outside his own studio in Oak Park, Illinois, and the roofline friezes on homes such as the Winslow, Dana, Heller, and Husser houses in Illinois were some of his significant decorative elements.

☐ Stucco. This durable, inexpensive building material was repeatedly used during the Prairie Style period. While it was most often seen in

Wright's designs for affordable housing such as the "Fireproof House for $5,000" of 1906 and the Richards American System Built Homes of 1916, it was employed also in numerous larger commissions, such as the William Martin and Fricke houses in Oak Park.

☐ Concrete. Once again, Wright looked at a lowly construction material, studied its properties, and made it beautiful. Lacking the inherent beauty of other materials, concrete was redeemed by its plasticity. It was poured into monolithic walls and cantilevered terraces. It was molded into tactile blocks. It was combined with steel to create a solid fabric. It was mixed with fine sand and large rocks to create natural panels. It was colored. It was poured as a floor, covering radiant heating systems. It was used as a roof. Wright shaped it and stretched it in countless ways in his buildings for more than fifty years.

☐ Copper. The decorative potential of copper, previously viewed primarily as a durable sheet metal, included color (from blue-green to bronze) and an inherent plasticity. Beginning with the horizontal stretch of the eaves, Wright wrapped this ancient material around other features, particularly near window expanses. Its liberal use in the Coonley house in Riverside, Illinois, and May house in Grand Rapids, Michigan, emphasized certain motifs and added richness to the overall designs. Pleated copper roofs were specified on several commissions, but they were not always built because of the cost and availability.

☐ Glass. Advances in glass technology, more than any other innovation, permitted Wright to break open the box. A foil for the texture and weight of other building materials, glass served to lighten Wright's designs. It enabled him to balance solid screens with light screens so that the building would no longer have to be confining. In the Prairie Style years, his intricate, geometric art glass designs repeated building colors and patterns and provided a privacy screen for the family within. The different facets of the glass reflected light in such a way that window coverings were unnecessary in the daytime. He discovered that when mitered at a corner, glass actually dissolved the intersection. When butted into a stone wall, glass served as protection from the weather while accenting the strength and texture of the stone. Used generously, glass allowed Wright to integrate inside and outside spaces, blurring the distinction between them.

Opposite, from left to right: Some of the key materials found in Wright's buildings: a limestone wall at Taliesin [Tony Puttnam, Frank Lloyd Wright Foundation]; tulip art glass at his Oak Park home [Gordon Beall]; a concrete textile block at the Ennis house [Balthazar Korab]; stucco on the Henderson house [© Judith Bromley]; brick at the Bogk house [Eric Oxendorf]; board-and-batten siding on the Davenport house [Chester Brummel]; limestone trim and common brick at Wright's home and studio [Ann Abernathy]; decorative copper gutters on the Dana-Thomas house [© Judith Bromley]; a rubble wall at Taliesin West [Richard Maack, Adstock].

COLOR

Wright selectively drew his color schemes from nature, leaning more towards the colors of autumn in the Midwest. The inherent colors of the building materials certainly dominated and set the tone for all of his decorative schemes. The warm tans and browns of the brick, stone, and wood usually were combined with varying shades of their component hues, from red to yellow-green, producing an analogous color scheme. Most often they ranged from a warm reddish gold to a muted yellow-green. Creams, beiges, warm grays, and browns were suitable additions. The colors were relatively intense but toned down enough not to be harsh. The appearance of an organic home was harmonious and restful, a unity of form and color. The palette might include several shades of the same basic colors that were varied throughout the house. There is a noticeable absence in Wright's repertoire of pure black and white; they seem to be in bold violation of his thesis of harmony and unity. Characteristic colors remained warm and autumnal for decades. Only in his later years, when others became more involved in the interiors, did occasional clear blues and chartreuse begin to appear in his homes.

Wright's use of red became his signature. In fact, red was the color of the square signature tile that he began to place on his houses in the 1930s. His long-time associate John Howe remembers that a client, one of the Pauson sisters, was a potter and suggested creating such a tile. Wright was delighted with the idea. While many reds were used in his schemes, he preferred a warm, brownish red that he called Cherokee red. Some say the color came from a favorite native American pot, but it could just as well have been inspired by the warm red barns that dotted his rural Wisconsin homeland. That red, actually an iron oxide mixture, was used to help preserve the wood in the barn. It was a familiar and natural companion to the colors of the foliage. Wright colored his own Midway farm buildings at Taliesin Cherokee red, as well as his fleet of cars, his roofs, his gates, and his signs. It was specified as the accent color in many of his buildings and continues to be generously used by his followers. Even concrete floors were integrally colored and waxed with a warm red.

The particular shade and intensity of red vary from site to site and use to use depending on the light, the building materials, and the setting. In practice, Cherokee red is not just one color but has become a range of hues. For instance, Taliesin West, Wright's home in Scottsdale, Arizona, uses a lighter value than Taliesin in Wisconsin. Paint pigmentation and composition have changed so dramatically since Wright first began his practice that now there is a hundred times more variety than before. For environmental and stability reasons, many of the natural pigments have been replaced with synthetics. But the ability to create a rich, brownish red is still a challenge.

Wright also experimented with metallic paints and gold leaf. Walls in his own Oak Park studio entrance were painted with a bronze paint; he even proposed gold leaf for the exterior of his masterpiece, Fallingwater. He was particularly fond of gold during his Imperial Hotel era in the late teens and 1920s, no doubt borrowing it from the Japanese screens he loved. Using different methods, he laid gold in the mortar joints of the brick fireplaces of the Martin house in Buffalo, May house in Grand Rapids, and Allen house in Wichita. Certainly a product of the earth, it added a richness, an elegance, that other materials could not.

Photographs, page 40, from left to right: Wright drew his colors from nature: a California sunrise [Don Giannatti, Adstock]; limestone outcroppings near Taliesin [Tony Puttnam, Frank Lloyd Wright Foundation]; sumac leaves in the fall [Balthazar Korab]; spring prairie grasses [Balthazar Korab].

Photographs, page 41, from left to right: Wrightian red showed itself in many hues: the trim of the bell at Taliesin West [Richard Bowditch]; Wright's 1940 Lincoln [Domino's Center for Architecture and Design]; the spiral Taliesin West logo [Richard Bowditch]; Wright's red signature tile at Taliesin [Richard Bowditch].

Opposite: Wrapping around a pier between the May house hall and dining room, a shimmering hollyhock mural draws on the golds and greens of the house's color palette. It was painted by George Niedecken, who coordinated the interiors, and was recently recovered from under six layers of paint. [John Boucher, Steelcase]

LIGHT

Both natural and artificial light were partners in Wright's harmonious whole. Houses were sited to make the most of the sun's powers. Window walls were most likely on the south elevation allowing the sun to flood the rooms with light and warmth. Skylights and clerestory windows brought natural light into rooms away from open window walls. The changing quality of light in different seasons and different times of day, controlled by the shape and location of his light screens, affected life in the home.

Electricity, introduced to the Chicago area at about the time Wright was building his first home in Oak Park, offered new opportunities for integrating lighting. It was now safe to conceal light behind grillework and art glass, reflect it off ceilings, and hang it over furniture. It could augment the sun's ability to create shadows and texture. For most of his career, Wright was fond of using decks—long, deep shelves that seemed to float below the ceiling—to hide indirect light fixtures, create spatial variety, and reduce the perceived height in a room to human scale. These decks, constructed of the same material as the ceiling, usually are on the perimeter of a space, but sometimes they span openings from one room to another.

Opposite: Wright carefully used natural light. He opened the southern facade of the May house to the sun, using art glass windows that wrap around the corner and rise to skylights overhead. They dissolve the wall and obliterate the corner. In the day a warm glow fills the room. [Jon Miller, © Hedrich-Blessing. Courtesy Steelcase]

Above: At dusk on a winter day, the skylight is illuminated and the wall and table lamps in the May house are turned on—creating a different, more dramatic, glow. The art glass uses square and abstract leaf motifs found throughout the house. [Balthazar Korab]

DECORATIVE ARTS

The majority of the decorative elements in a Wright environment are designed to be part of the unified whole. Wright liked to integrate all of the arts. Furniture, light fixtures, carpets, fireplace andirons, sometimes linens and china often were augmented by sculpture, decorative grilles, screens, and murals designed for that particular site. George Niedecken, who coordinated many of Wright's interiors during the heyday of the Prairie Style years, began working with Wright as a muralist. His paintings of plants and flowers were used on the upper walls of several major commissions including the Dana, Coonley, and May residences. Marion Mahony, the only woman designer in the Oak Park studio, also was responsible for many of the early decorative art designs. Later, Gene Masselink provided masterful geometric murals that became focal points of Wright interiors. Japanese screens were sometimes recommended to clients and would be attached to or built into a wall. Perforated wood panels or concrete blocks in abstracted nature patterns were used as screens for natural and artificial light. Two outstanding examples of ceiling grilles are in Wright's Oak Park home, one in the playroom and the other in the dining room (page 17). Nearly every Usonian house had its own geometric, perforated grille pattern that created shadows in the appropriate motif throughout the home.

Right: The art glass skylight in Wright's Oak Park studio is one of his most complex designs. He used such panels in ceilings and windows as decorative elements, as a means of diffusing light, and as a visual picture frame. Their varied facets reflect light during the day so that windows can be uncovered yet private. [Chester Brummel]

Opposite, left to right: A montage of decorative arts from Wright's creative treasury: scumbling, a multiple-step painting technique, Dana-Thomas house [© Judith Bromley]; brick fireplace with golden glass in the mortar joints, May house [John Boucher, Steelcase]; textured upholstery fabric, Zimmerman house [Michael Komanecky]; lighted textile block, Freeman house [John Marshall]; bronze sconce, May house [John Boucher, Steelcase]; Sullivanesque master bedroom stencil detail, Wright's Oak Park home [Chester Brummel]; geometric carpet design, May house [John Boucher, Steelcase]; dining room chair, Wright's Oak Park home [© Judith Bromley]; plywood Usonian furniture detail, Zimmerman house [Michael Komanecky].

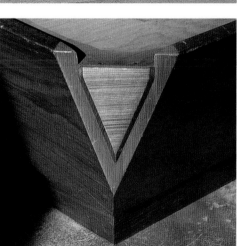

FURNITURE

Wright began to design furniture for his buildings as he was formu-
lating his concepts of organic architecture. First, in the 1880s and
1890s, he adopted the conventional mode by building in some
cabinets and shelving. Soon he added seating units around fireplaces
and in hallways. Then in 1895 he designed his own dining room table
and chairs, possibly his first free-standing furniture. His concept of a
totally integrated, harmonious interior required that he design more
and more furniture for his buildings, because there was little on the
market that had the rectilinear simplicity required to fulfill his vision.
But the extent to which Wright actually designed pieces for the early
houses varied, probably based on the willingness of clients to either
spend the money or submit to his ideas.

In some of the Prairie houses, he designed built-in cabinets
and possibly a bench, a large dining or library table, and maybe
some chairs. These would be mixed with more ornate pieces owned
by the client. As his concepts and his ability to persuade clients
matured, he was able to design more and more elements so that the
furniture was barely distinguishable from the building itself, as can be
seen in the later Prairie and Usonian houses; the furniture was made
of the same materials, same finishes, same details and proportions.
The clients who moved into his houses often were forced to leave
their old furniture behind. They neither needed it nor wanted it to
interfere with the unity of their new homes.

His furniture styles thus evolved, just as his architectural
vocabulary changed. The solid rectilinear oak pieces of the Prairie era
became lighter and then more Oriental in feeling as his architectural
interests shifted. The economical simplicity of the Usonian houses
called for basic furniture, built of plywood, presumably constructed
on site by the carpenters but usually by local cabinetmakers. The versatility of the pieces, in addition to their inherent suitablity to the
spaces, makes it hard to imagine one without the other.

In 1955 Wright created a line of furniture for the Heritage-
Henredon Furniture Company, thus opening his creativity to those
who did not own a Wright-designed home. While this may seem to
be a compromise in his ideals, the line was based on the same principles as his house-specific furniture. Using basic circular, rectilinear, and
triangular shapes, most of the seventy-five mahogany pieces were
modular, so that they could adapt to different settings. They were
simple and functional, with the ornament integral—not applied to it.

TEXTILES

Textiles that Wright selected were simple and natural—no heavy brocades or elaborate floral prints. Instead, he preferred simple linens, cottons, and wools in flat weaves or fine, short-napped velvets. He was known to assist in the actual design of a particular weave of upholstery or drapery fabric. Textiles were used to complement or accentuate the surrounding texture of a room. In the first few decades, satin-weave wools, velvets, and tightly woven linens seemed to be the dominant choices. Eventually, more handwoven and nubbier textures provided contrast for the smoother Usonian houses. When a pattern was used, it was geometric and related to the overall motif of the building. Leather was a popular chair covering, and an occasional animal skin was added to provide variety in textures. Each textile became one more unit that contributed to the integrity of the whole.

Influenced by the Arts and Crafts movement near the turn of the century, and encouraged by the needlework ability of the wife of one of his designers, George Niedecken, Wright included custom-designed linens in several of his Prairie Style houses. Patterns used in the table and bed scarves again were drawn from the house's dominating geometric motif.

Carpets and floor coverings also were simple and made of natural fibers. Wright or one of his associates, such as George Niedecken or Marion Mahony, custom designed woven carpets for some of the Prairie houses. As part of the unified whole, they served to pull together the geometric motifs and colors that were used elsewhere in the home. Current reproductions are often tufted but, if properly done, can provide the same appearance as the historic weaves. In some of the later homes, woven linen, jute, and wool mats were chosen, providing a textured foil for the smooth concrete floors. Geometric Oriental, native American, and Scandinavian rugs and weavings also were widely used, allowing owners to personalize their homes with their textile collections.

The 1908 Robie house commission gave Wright the opportunity to design many decorative arts, including numerous pieces of oak furniture and carpeting. The shape of the sofa, with its unique table arms, echoes the ceiling above it. The trim on the furniture matches the moldings on the walls, creating free-standing architectural elements in a totally unified space. [Jon Miller, © Hedrich-Blessing]

ACCESSORIES

Free-standing accessories most compatible with Wright interiors tend to be somewhat geometric and nature oriented. Tree branches and boughs, usually evergreens, are brought inside and spread overhead across light decks, on shelves, and on tabletops in both of Wright's Taliesins. Simple, natural bouquets of seasonal flowers or dried weeds fill geometric vases. Arts and Crafts, native American, pre-Columbian, and contemporary pottery fit easily into his geometric schemes. Certain Arts and Crafts ceramics and metalware also work comfortably in a Wright interior. Items with solid matte finishes and geometric shapes are most compatible. The blue-green color of Teco pottery is a nice complement to the warm tones preferred by the architect.

Wright-designed spaces can accommodate sculptures more readily than paintings because of the limited amount of open wall space. This deliberate rejection of most two-dimensional art excluded his beloved Japanese prints, which he stored and exhibited on specially designed print tables or easels.

Wright's care in selecting accessories was the culmination of the attention he gave to every aspect of his houses, from fitting the form to the site, selecting the materials, and using natural inspirations wherever he found them. His organic architecture speaks to the values of today's society even more accurately than it did at the turn of the century. In a hectic, complex, impersonal world that is being forced to look at the lessons of nature to save the planet, there is great relevance in Wright's teachings. His designs were based on simplicity, the dignity of the individual, and, above all, an abiding respect for nature.

At the Dana house, Wright called on Richard Bock to provide sculptures to suit the grand spaces. Bock's *The Flower in the Crannied Wall* stands at the entry, greeting guests. Wright worked closely with Bock, Alfonso Iannelli, and George Niedecken in his early years to integrate works of art into his houses. [© Judith Bromley]

Opposite: At the Hollyhock house, the Los Angeles residence Wright designed for arts patron Aline Barnsdall, he created decorative wooden torchieres as part of the sofa. Behind the high-back chair is a Japanese screen, one of his favorite accessories; its metallic gold background is repeated in the wall finish. [© Alexander Vertikoff]

WRIGHT'S OWN HOMES

THERE IS NO BETTER WAY TO EXPERIENCE THE GENIUS OF WRIGHT'S DESIGN ABILITY THAN TO EXPLORE THE PLACES IN WHICH HE LIVED. HIS THREE HOMES STAND AS COMPLETE EXPRESSIONS OF ORGANIC ARCHITECTURE — FROM THREE PERSPECTIVES OF THE MASTER HIMSELF.

Previous pages: A blazing fire in one of many fireplaces at Taliesin, Wright's Wisconsin home, conveys the power of the hearth—the center of Wright houses. Here, tea is prepared for guests on a cool afternoon. The gnarled driftwood and wrought-iron fixtures, so carefully placed, complete the cavelike setting. [Richard Bowditch]

Opposite: Client presentations were made in the octagonal library in Wright's Oak Park studio. Here, protected from distraction, in a deliberately controlled space, he held clients in rapt attention. The unity of the space, with its oak furniture and selected artifacts, was an advertisement for his creativity. [Jon Miller, © Hedrich-Blessing]

HOME AND STUDIO

In 1889 twenty-one-year-old Frank Lloyd Wright borrowed $5,000 from his employer, Louis Sullivan, to build a six-room bungalow for himself and his new eighteen-year-old bride, Catherine Tobin. For the next twenty years, he shaped this building in Oak Park, Illinois, in response to the changing needs of his family and his emerging design philosophy. Like his future homes, Taliesin and Taliesin West, it became his laboratory. Here he could safely experiment with new concepts that he further developed in his commissions.

While compact, the house already discloses Wright's desire to break out of traditional boxlike rooms. Doorways were widened or eliminated so space could flow freely, allowing the rooms to seem larger and less confining. Simple oak bands wrap around the walls, leading the eye from room to room and providing a human scale.

The walls of the house conveyed the feeling of movable screens rather than solid walls, even before the Japanese pavilion at the Columbian Exposition in 1893 could have affected his attitude toward space. These solid screens, contrasted with window groupings that serve as light screens, make the living spaces feel flexible and open, suitable for a growing family's needs. Wright had not begun to design his own art glass windows when the house was built. Thus, he selected a simple geometric diamond pattern that created only a minor transitional barrier between the inside and the outside. The walls were starting to dissolve.

Frank and Catherine furnished their home with antiques bought at auctions in the area until Wright began to design his own furniture. A mixture of exotic wood tables and cabinets, an upright piano, palms, and a patchwork of Oriental rugs fill the rooms. Velvet upholstered built-in seating areas are beneath the windows. The family's exuberance was apparent in their unconventional home.

By 1895 the Wrights had four active children who needed more space. A large addition was built adjoining the east side of the house. It includes two brilliantly articulated and integrated spaces: the barrel-vaulted playroom (pages 6–7) and a new dining room (page 17) where the former kitchen had been. These new rooms demonstrated how far Wright had come artistically in just six years. His principles of organic architecture, written the year before, were firmly in place. The rooms were functionally responsive, geometrically pure, and partners with nature. Both have wooden fretwork panels in the ceiling in abstracted nature patterns. The playroom screen has a skylight, and the dining room has a recessed electric light, a first. Like branches overhead, they shelter but open the spaces above. The light fixtures and furniture were built as components of the architecture. It is totally unified environment. Other spaces on both floors shifted their uses slightly now that the family could stretch out a bit. The old dining room became the study. Wright's studio became the bedroom for all of the children.

Within three years Wright decided to integrate his work and home life. The studio addition was constructed, advertising his revolutionary ideas to all. To the triangular-shaped home he added a complex, geometric composition of rectangles, octagons, and squares. It includes a drafting room with a balcony, his office, a library, and an impressive reception hall. Long, low brick walls stretch across the entire facade, unifying all of the elements. Two sculptures of bent human figures, columns with integrated molded plaster panels, and huge planted urns designate the mazelike entrance (page 35).

The richness continues inside the studio. The low ceiling of the metallic bronze-colored reception hall includes three long, intricate art glass panels (page 44). Light filters through their gold and green geometric designs, abstractions from nature. To the left is the octagonal drafting room, and to the right is the octagonal library. Straight ahead is Wright's office, where art glass panels filter natural light from overhead and frame a garden view. Everywhere one looks are stimulating new architectural ideas and lush decorative arts.

Today, the restored spaces appear just as they were when Wright lived and worked there. The building now is owned by the National Trust for Historic Preservation and operated by the Frank Lloyd Wright Home and Studio Foundation.

Above: Seen here from the study, the living room is light-filled from expanses of simple diamond-paned windows or "light screens." Wright streamlined the furnishings with built-in seats. The colors—like the earth itself—are darker at the base and lighten as the eye moves upward, from oak to cream. [Jon Miller, © Hedrich-Blessing]

Opposite below: The original six-room, Shingle Style bungalow, with its sheltering roof and extended garden wall, was later joined by the studio at left. [Donald G. Kalec]

Left: The inglenook presides over an intimate alcove, a contrast to the overall feeling of spaciousness. A polygonal cabinet echoes nearby bay windows. [Chester Brummel]

Studio activity centered on the two-story drafting room. An octagon on a cube, with a balcony suspended by chains above the work area, it was revolutionary in its space and materials. Here Wright and his eager apprentices poured out 162 building designs over thirteen whirlwind years. [Jon Miller, © Hedrich-Blessing]

Earth tones in Wright's studio office created a muted yet welcoming retreat. Natural light, diffused through colored panels, came in from a skylight overhead and art glass windows to the side. The straight lines of the modern chair contrast nicely with Japanese prints, textiles, and dried weeds in pottery vases. [Chester Brummel]

TALIESIN

Wright left the Oak Park home in 1909, first traveling to Europe to assist with the publication of his work by German publisher Ernst Wasmuth. A former client, Mamah Borthwick Cheney, accompanied him. Both had decided to leave their spouses and begin a new chapter in their lives. On his return to the United States two years later, Anna Lloyd Wright convinced her son that he should take over her property near the family enclave in Spring Green, Wisconsin.

In 1911 he began plans for a home there that would be "of the hill, not on the hill," one that overlooked the Wisconsin River and the land of his Welsh forebears. He named it Taliesin, which means "shining brow" in Welsh and was also the name of a famous Welsh poet. Taliesin was designed to be a self-sufficient farm, not just a home. The limestone and sand-colored stucco walls stretched across the hill, enclosing farm buildings, studio space, and courtyards as well as living space. This was the beginning of a remarkable complex that suffered several major fires and was rebuilt and remodeled continuously as Wright perfected his own environment over the next forty-eight years.

Today, Taliesin is a beautifully created community of organic buildings. The original home and studio of approximately 7,000 square feet have grown to some 37,000 square feet, plus three-quarters as much in gardens, courts, and terraces. Nestled neatly, under broad sheltering roofs, on other parts of the 600 rolling acres are the Hillside Home School buildings, Tan-y-deri (his sister's house), several other smaller residences, the Midway farm buildings, and the Romeo and Juliet windmill (a Wright design from 1896). A dammed-up stream on the valley floor creates a waterfall and pond 100 feet below the home. Surrounding vegetable gardens provide food for the Taliesin Fellowship, an apprenticeship-based architecture school that still resides at Taliesin, particularly during the warm months.

The house is really a series of connected buildings joined by roofed passageways and courtyards. The transition from outside to inside is smooth and deliberate. The covered courtyard at the entrance gradually becomes the foyer within the home, the limestone floor continuing. Once inside, the compressed foyer space is released into the great expanse of the living room to the left. The ceiling follows the roofline two stories up, but the room is decidedly horizontal and tranquil in feeling. The interplay of spaces, textures, light, and color draws one into the room. New discoveries are around

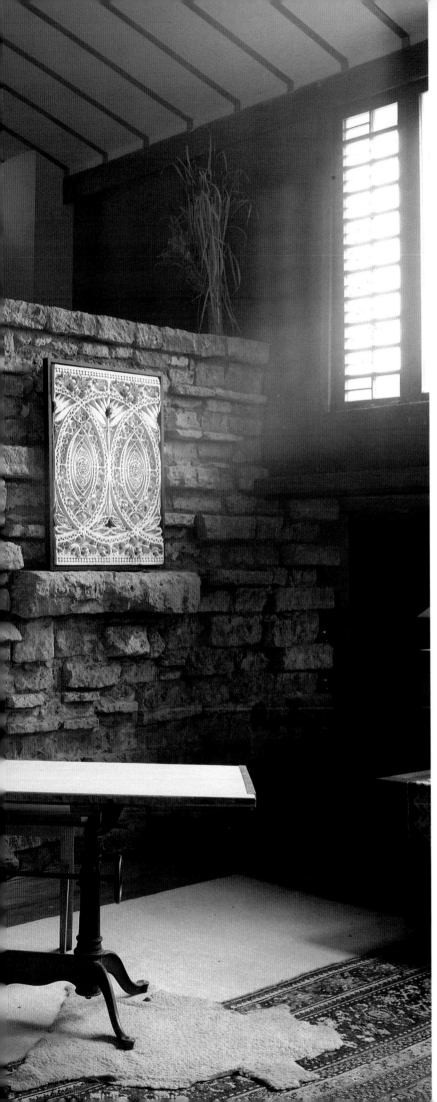

each corner: a massive fireplace, a tiny alcove, a place to sit and reflect, a place to listen to music, a place to visit with friends.

A narrow, forty-foot balcony is cantilevered into the treetops for better viewing of the natural life below. The limestone walls, where exposed, are laid with alternating rows of projecting stones, like the quarries from which they came. The sand and golden plaster walls are divided by cypress bands into horizontal panels that serve as backdrops for a panoply of decorative arts. The geometry of the custom-designed furniture, art glass, and carpets complements the natural vistas framed by the windows (pages 4–5). Selected pieces of Oriental art are scattered throughout Taliesin, some actually cemented into place as permanent, integral parts of the building.

To the right of the foyer flow a guest room, a loggia, a garden room, and private bedrooms of the Wrights. Above and below are more guest quarters. Each room has a thoughtfully crafted fireplace on a principal wall. These are the only heat sources for most of the building but serve to radiate the essential beauty of the stone as much as the heat. Most of the openings are vertical or oversized. In some the top stone is laid on its side; others are open from two sides. Ceiling heights change from room to room, redefining the spaces for their particular use. Doors and windows frequently open onto balconies, cantilevered observation decks, or terraces, continuing the flow of space. Most of the rooms are oriented to the east, bringing the morning light into the composition. The harmony within each room and among rooms leaves a feeling of inner tranquility.

Wright's studio adjoins the home through a covered walkway. It was his private atelier, where he welcomed clients and discussed his visions that would change their lives. A decorative panel from Sullivan's Auditorium Building hangs on the limestone wall, and a Buddha looks on from above. Natural grasses brought in from the surrounding field fill earthen pots. [Richard Bowditch]

Following pages: The living room is one of the most memorable spaces in America. The drama of its soaring multilevel spaces; the tactile variety of the stone, plaster, and wood surfaces; the artistry in the furniture; the golden tones; the genius of the composition are all intrinsically Wrightian. Barrel chairs repeat circular shapes in the carpet beneath them. [© Yukio Futagawa]

Above: The garden court, created of geometric limestone ornamented with colorful vegetation, includes a tea circle beneath an ancient oak tree. In this outdoor room the Wrights gathered with their apprentices and guests for afternoon tea. It was a restful space that conveyed his most elemental beliefs in the power of simplicity, geometry, and nature. [Balthazar Korab]

Left: The garden gate, made of iron pipe painted Cherokee red, is a linear composition that serves as a counterpoint to vines and flowers. [Richard Bowditch]

Opposite: From across a pond, the earth-colored Taliesin appears out of the greenery like a treehouse. Designed to be *of* the hill, not *on* it, the long, low building stretches across the brow of the hill. From its rooms, Wright could view the rolling river valley farms that were settled by his forebears. Reflected in the water, Taliesin seems at one with nature. Apprentices of the Taliesin Fellowship, founded here in 1932, work down the hill in the large drafting room that once was the Hillside Home School, which Wright's aunts had operated. [Richard Bowditch]

TALIE∫IN WE∫T

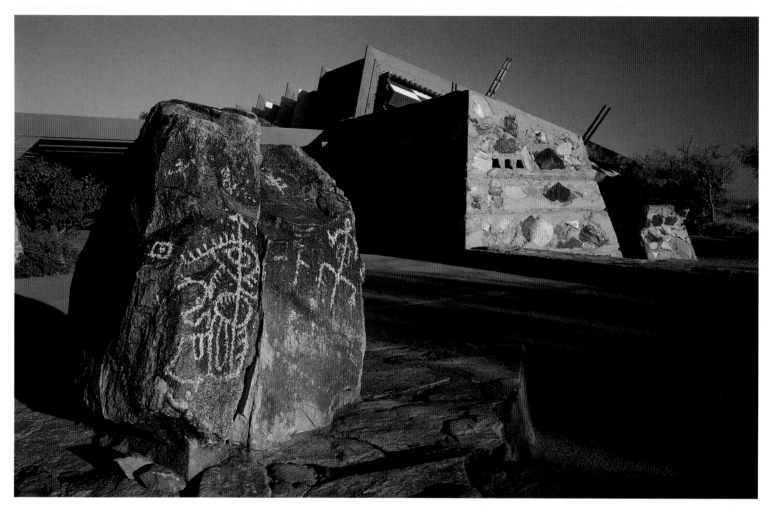

By 1932 Wright had founded the Taliesin Fellowship, whose apprentices shared all aspects of life at Taliesin. Cooking, gardening, scrubbing, partying, playing music, and entertaining were all as much a part of the communal life as the architectural tasks. Like Wright's spaces, his unified lifestyle did not compartmentalize daily life. Wright and his third wife, Olgivanna, decided in 1937 that the Wisconsin winters were too unbearable for year-round occupancy. Taliesin was not centrally heated and thus was insufferable in the subzero cold.

In 1928 Wright and some apprentices built near Phoenix, Arizona, a canvas-covered camp, Ocatillo, that in some ways became the prototype for Taliesin West. They later found a beautiful mesa just below McDowell Peak near Scottsdale that was perfect for their permanent architectural camp. Construction of the winter home for the fellowship, which then numbered about thirty people, began in 1937.

Wright described Taliesin West in his 1943 autobiography.

Plans were inspired by the character and beauty of that wonderful site. . . . Just imagine what it would be like on top of the world looking over the Universe at sunrise or at sunset with clear sky in between. Light and air bathing all the worlds of creation in all the color that ever was— all the shapes and outlines ever devised . . . all beyond the reach of the human mind. . . . For the designing of our buildings, certain forms already abounded. There were simple characteristic silhouettes to go by, tremendous drifts and heaps of sunburned desert rocks were nearby to be used. . . . From first to last, thousands of cords of stone, carloads of cement, carloads of redwood, acres of stout white canvas doubled over wood frames four feet by eight feet. . . . We devised a light canvas covered redwood framework resting upon this massive stone masonry that belonged to the mountain slopes all around. On a fair day, when these white tops and side flaps were flung open, the desert air and the birds flew clear through.

Opposite: Wright's western retreat drew its triangular motif from the surrounding mountain profiles, a unity of building and site. The solidity of the masonry base contrasts with the airiness of the top. Appearing both anchored and adrift, the good ship Taliesin West projects confidence and adventure. Ancient boulders with native American petroglyphs were relocated to prominent places. [Richard Maack, Adstock]

Left: The patterns of the angular redwood forms are most apparent in the drafting room, now covered with plastic. [Balthazar Korab]

Following pages: The garden room was used by the family, for fellowship gatherings, for a constant stream of guests, and for frequent musical concerts. The "butterfly" chairs, like folded origami, repeat the triangular theme of the room. [© Yukio Futagawa]

Like Taliesin, Taliesin West was ever-evolving and changed as the needs of the fellowship changed. The canvas roofs were rearranged, rebuilt, and eventually replaced with various synthetic materials that were more durable but permitted the same translucent light. Glass, not allowed in the early plans, was added in greater and greater quantities beginning in 1945. Spaces were added and made more permanent. Three rooms—Wright's private office, the drafting room, and the garden room—were the original canvas-covered spaces. They joined a dining room, a kitchen, Wright's private quarters to the east, and an apprentices court to the north.

Also like Taliesin, Taliesin West is actually many separate buildings linked together by partially covered walkways, courtyards, and terraces, all surrounded by native vegetation. Moving through the complex, one is guided, but not controlled. Even the steps are gentle,

broad, and shallow, more horizontal than vertical. Shadows link the architectural elements and furniture, repeating the angular, rhythmic lines of the mountains behind. The trellised pergola along the drafting room leaves a pattern on the ground below. The natural colors, from mauve to an orange-red, are accentuated by the blooming vegetation. This does not appear to be a barren desert but a lush one, rich with natural wonders, enhanced by skillful management of its resources.

Everywhere, breathtaking vistas and fascinating close-up views are framed. The rugged textures and open informal spaces seem both primitive, like the original camp, and yet sophisticated. The contrasts abound: the simplicity and the grandeur; the smooth and the rough; the light and the heavy; the narrow and the expansive; the regular and the irregular, the natural and the built; cool blue with warm pinks. Each element was made greater by the other.

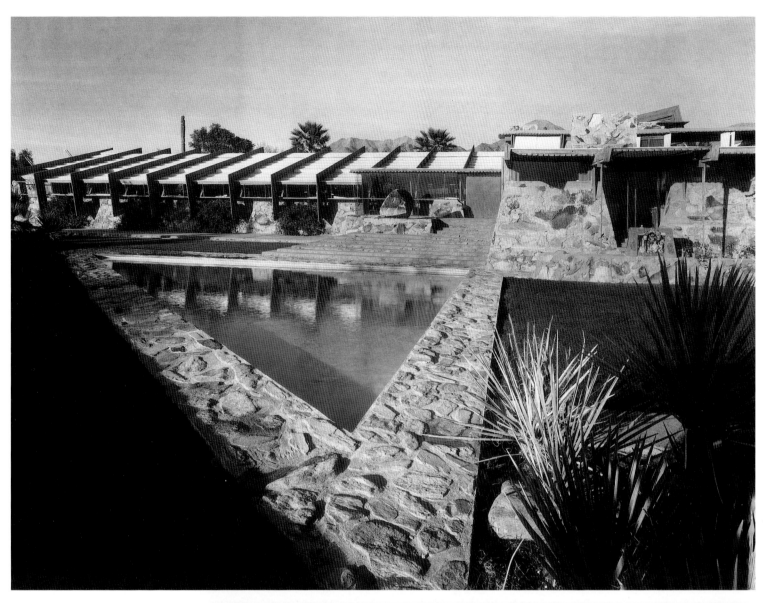

Above: Water—splashing, cooling, reflecting—became an integral design element here, a dramatic and soothing contrast to the desert dryness. The triangular pool repeats the complex's main theme. This 1937 view shows the camplike winter headquarters soon after it was built. [Hedrich-Blessing, Chicago Historical Society]

Opposite and right: The unusual, battered rubble walls, inside and out, were created because all of the large desert stones seemed to have one flat side. Rather than cut them to shape, Wright—always experimenting—decided to use their flat, colorful side out, sideways, in a bed of formed concrete. [Ezra Stoller, © Esto]

CLASSIC WRIGHT HOUSES

WHETHER DESIGNED TO ALIGN WITH THE PRAIRIE, PROJECT OVER A WATERFALL, RECALL ANCIENT MAYANS, OR PROVIDE AN ECONOMICAL HOME PERFECT FOR AMERICAN LIVING — THESE CLASSIC HOUSES CONVEY THE ESSENCE OF THE ENVIRONMENTS WRIGHT CREATED.

Opposite: Wright gave Susan Lawrence Dana an extraordinary dining room and gallery in which to entertain governors, politicians, and other notable guests. The dramatic barrel-vaulted ceiling in the Springfield, Illinois, house repeats the grand arch over the main entry. A stylized mural of sumac and other foliage, painted by George Niedecken, surrounds the upper walls of the dining room, furthering the feeling of being in a forest glen—with lights as fanciful as butterflies. Sometimes as many as forty chairs were grouped around the dining table, alternating high and low versions and creating a mini-room within the larger room. Here as elsewhere in the house, special benches invited one to sit in more intimate areas. Print tables allowed close study of art in the gallery. Music was always a lively ingredient of Dana's dinners, parties, and charitable events. When the house was commissioned in 1902, it was the largest residence Wright had ever undertaken. [© Judith Bromley]

PRAIRIE STYLE

Wright's early experiments with historic styles and his life experiences coalesced into a grammar of forms that became known as the Prairie School of architecture—not an education center but a school of thought. The Prairie Style was an attempt by Wright and a group of other young Chicago architects to create an architecture that suited the American lifestyle and landscape. Louis Sullivan contributed much of the initial philosophical enthusiasm, but Wright was the most famous Prairie School practitioner.

Some say that the style was definitively launched by the publication of Wright's design for "A Home in a Prairie Town" in the *Ladies' Home Journal* in February 1901. This strongly horizontal plan for a house with a low sheltering roof, bands of art glass windows, stucco walls with wood banding, and outreaching garden walls had many of the features that characterized this version of Wright's organic architecture. In one of his first commissions after this plan was published, the house for Susan Lawrence Dana, Wright brought to bear most of the devices he ultimately used to express organic architecture. For the next ten years he refined, refitted, and reinterpreted this memorable style in scores of residences. After that, it no longer dominated his architectural designs, but the grammar was not lost. Even Lucille and Isadore Zimmerman's house of 1950 exhibits many Prairie Style elements.

Over time most of the following Prairie Style houses, designed in Wright's early years, have maintained, or retained through authentic restorations, their purity and unity.

The May house in Grand Rapids, Michigan, one of Wright's mature Prairie designs, incorporates all of the components of the style. The architecture expresses the open, enchanting spaces within the home. The low-pitched roof, broad overhanging eaves, and linear masonry walls anchor the building to its site. But Wright proceeded to engage the land even more by recessing the home eighteen inches below grade and further shortening the perceived building height with a knee-high hedge on the earthen berms. Garden walls, planters, terraces, and balconies stretch the interior spaces beyond their walls. Bold geometric details around the windows is reminiscent of Mayan forms. Squares within squares are wrapped in bronze-toned copper. [Jon Miller, © Hedrich-Blessing. Courtesy Steelcase]

DANA-THOMAS HOUSE

Susan Lawrence Dana, a wealthy heiress and recent widow, commissioned Wright to create an extravagant place for living and entertaining in Springfield, Illinois. The resulting thirty-five-room mansion, completed in 1904, was an imaginative and complex symphony of color and form.

Strong geometric shapes introduced outside (pages 26–27) are a preview of the varied spaces on the interior. And varied they are: ceiling levels that change dramatically within rooms, compressing then releasing; balconies to look up at and down from; hidden alcoves and nooks to be discovered; stages for musicians; a bowling alley and a billiard room. Imagination and adventure are everywhere. Generous wood bands wrap up, down, and around the walls and sometimes span spaces as light decks to further define and unite the areas. Every space, every surface, every view is carefully composed to be a unified part of the luscious whole.

Inside is a magical kingdom. Intricate art glass sparkles all around, creating subtle screens. The complex interplay of thousands of facets of glass produces a reflected light that makes the house appear jewel-like. Autumnal colors used in the glass were applied also to the textured plaster walls with a multiple-step process called scumbling, which left the walls mottled like dappled sunlight, intensifying the glow of the spaces (page 9). Tawny golds, olive greens, and burnished oranges are paired with an unusually reddish stain on the wood. It is polychromatic yet retains a unified tonal quality like a forest on a sunny fall day. In the absence of natural vegetation on the site, Wright chose to be particularly effusive with his ornament.

Dana left her home in 1928, and it remained empty until purchased by the Thomas Publishing Company in 1944. Now owned by the state of Illinois, it has been meticulously brought back to life.

The solid, rectilinear furniture echoes the scale and proportions of the rooms. Oak tables and seating pieces are trimmed and finished in the same manner as the wood moldings on the walls and ceilings. Nearly a hundred furniture pieces were designed, along with carpets, sculptures (page 49), and murals. [© Judith Bromley]

Following pages: The principal windows in the house are a geometric interpretation of sumac, whose angular shapes became the unifying theme for all of the art glass designs. The generous budget permitted four hundred fifty custom-designed art glass panels and two hundred light fixtures. [© Yukio Futagawa]

MARTIN HOUSE

Between 1902 and 1904, Wright managed to break away from Sulli-vanesque ornamentation and simplify his designs even more. The Darwin D. Martin residence in Buffalo, New York, while a more elaborate commission than the Dana house, was less lavishly ornamented. This entire complex for the president of the Larkin Company included a house for his sister and brother-in-law, as well as the Martins' home, garage, and conservatory. Introduced to Wright by his brother, William Martin, an Oak Park client, Darwin Martin became one of Wright's greatest patrons. Over the years, the Martin brothers were responsible for nine major commissions. Darwin Martin also responded to Wright's periodic financial troubles with some desperately needed cash at crucial times.

The Martin house spaces are purely rectilinear, based on a strict, rectangular unit of design. Every element of the composition—windows, walls, furniture, floor plan, piers, moldings—repeats the same proportions, creating an internal, harmonious rhythm. Here Wright truly broke out of the box. Only the lower half of the exterior window walls outlines the building's shape. The low-pitch, hipped roofs float above, with only a shadow leading to the set-back

windows beneath them. Strong vertical brick piers on the facade support the broad stretches of roof, freeing the walls from any structural responsibility. Standing like sentinels, they point to the dominant horizontality of the design.

Inside, more Roman brick piers support light decks that stretch from room to room, passing and intersecting the complex pattern of finely detailed wood moldings (page 33). The gold-filled, deeply raked mortar joints of the brickwork reflect light, floating the courses of brick one above the other. All first-floor living spaces open generously into each other, offering long views from one to another. Through exquisite geometric windows, natural life in the garden, oversized planters, and the conservatory could be viewed—some nearby, some at a distance.

Wright produced dozens of custom furnishing designs for the Martins, including light fixtures, rugs, and even a grand piano. Most of the sturdy oak pieces repeated the dominant rectangular theme, but the circle became an important counterpoint. While loyal to his rectangular module, Wright had an uncanny sense about the need for variety and contrast to provide relief.

The Martins shared Wright's love of nature. He gave them a conservatory and pergola, both now lost, and niches for greenery such as this typically Wrightian urn with flowers. Many art glass patterns once graced windows, doors, and skylights, only some of which remain today. The State University of New York at Buffalo has owned the house for twenty-five years and is pursuing a complete restoration. [Balthazar Korab]

Opposite: The bold arch of the reception room fireplace repeats the curve motif and draws one to the warmth and intimacy of this secondary living room space. Wright used the same barrel chairs at his home Taliesin and at Wingspread, his house for Herbert Johnson in Wisconsin. Warm brown tones of the Roman brick blend with the golden oak and yellow, gold, and amber of the fabrics. [K. C. Kratt]

MAY HOUSE

Wright's commissions were not all as grand as the Dana and Martin houses. Most were for middle-class business people who had a sense of adventure but a more modest budget. When Grand Rapids, Michigan, clothier Meyer May and his wife, Sophie, contracted with Wright to design them a home in 1908, they were rewarded with a Prairie Style gem. In part because of the able assistance of designer George Niedecken, it was as thoroughly detailed as any of the larger residences.

Sunlight pours into the living areas through generous banks of art glass windows all across the southern facade, throwing geometric light patterns into the room (pages 42–43). The interior spaces open freely, one to another, with interesting transitions. They practically glow. The rich, golden tones—dominated by the natural color of the oak trim, floors, and furniture—are totally harmonious. Values shift easily from tan to brownish orange to tawny golds to pale yellow-greens. But there is relief from this limited palette. A bit of gray-blue sets off the carpet colors, and an uncharacteristic pink is offered in a Niedecken mural (page 39). The art glass in the windows, ceiling panels, cabinet doors, and even the fireplace mortar

joints (page 45) continue the golden theme. The mass glistens and lightens with the reflection from the windows across the room.

Squares and abstracted leaf forms are repeated in the carpet patterns, art glass, and embroidered linen patterns. Like members of a family, they all share a genetic commonality. Wright-designed furniture was supplemented in the bedrooms by Arts and Crafts pieces, especially Stickley items. The simple, sturdy shapes blend easily with the spaces and the Wright components.

Light fixtures also were specially designed to be part of the unified whole. Wall sconces like those in other Prairie Style homes are placed in banded panels throughout the main floor, but custom lamps for particular spaces also were fabricated. All use the colored art glass found in the windows. In the living room, cove lighting reflected off the ceiling provides a soft light for a harmonious room.

Within fourteen years of its construction, a large addition became the first of many changes that drastically altered the house over the years. In 1985 it was authentically restored by its new owner, Steelcase Inc. Today, it is possible to experience once again Wright's perfectly unified living environment.

Opposite: When seated in the dining room, guests could see the outdoor garden through geometric art glass on one side and a mural garden on the other side.

Left: In the master bedroom is a smaller but similar version of the golden fireplace in the living room.

Following pages: The living room furniture is more upholstered than in many of Wright's earlier homes. A slight flare at the foot of all seating and cabinet pieces, while unusual in his furniture of the period, breaks the monotony of the straight line. But the principal motif is clearly rectilinear. [Photographs by Jon Miller, © Hedrich-Blessing. Courtesy Steelcase]

LITTLE HOUSE II

Wright had already designed another home for Mr. and Mrs Francis W. Little in Peoria, Illinois, when they approached him about a new house on Lake Minnetonka in Wayzata, outside Minneapolis. Northome became one of his last Prairie Style houses when it was completed in 1914.

The living room, by far the dominant space in the house, is nearly fifty feet long. Mrs. Little was an accomplished musician and wanted the room to double as a recital space. The height of the ceiling adds to the room's grandeur. Flanked by two long walls with more than a dozen art glass windows on two levels, the room has the lightness of an outdoor pavilion. Clear glass was used in the leaded panels so that the magnificent views—the lake was to one side and the woods to the other—would not be obstructed. The delicate designs of lines and triangles, concentrated on the outer edges of the window, reach across several panels, creating a larger composition than on just the one window. The art glass skylights, an intricate checkerboard of tiny squares and triangles, are framed by heavy wood moldings.

The Littles brought some furniture from their 1903 house to their new home, and Wright augmented it with additional designs.

The rectilinear Prairie Style furniture had changed little over the decade, so that the sturdy oak shapes of tables, cabinets, and chairs adapted easily to the house's scale. The vertical spindles of the radiator covers are repeated in the base of the print table and seem to capture the rhythm of the wood marking strips across the ceiling. The strong horizontality of the entire house and the room itself pulls the scale back down to a more human level.

Foliage of the season is brought inside to fill oversized vases. *Winged Victory*, Wright's favorite classical sculpture, rises from a table top. Oriental carpets were used occasionally to add pattern to otherwise solid tones of golds and browns. Each detail contributed to the serenity of the home.

In 1972 the Little family decided to build a new house on the site. Learning that the original home would be demolished, the Metropolitan Museum of Art in New York offered to document the dismantling and purchase the parts. The living room was then rebuilt as part of the museum's American Wing. Other rooms were sold to museums and collectors. While this fragmentation is tragic and antithetical to Wright's concept of unity, it does provide an opportunity for millions of visitors to experience the interior of a Wright house.

Opposite: The living room was the grandest space in the sprawling Prairie Style house. Reconstructed in the Metropolitan Museum of Art in New York, the room's transition from a natural site to a museum setting has refocused the perception of this space as an art object. Still compelling are the linear power of the light screens, the mastery of scale and proportion, the delicate strength of the wood spindles, the subtle contrasts in color and pattern, the variety and unity within the space. Yet the original intended use of the room, as a recital space and family gathering area, prevails as the source of the room's masterful design. [Ping Amranand]

CALIFORNIA HOUSES

The 1920s were sparse years for Wright's career. His private life was chaotic, and between 1916 and 1922 he traveled back and forth to Japan, living there for long periods while supervising construction of the Imperial Hotel and a few other commissions. Despite his inattention to his practice in the United States, Wright created a group of exciting buildings in California, hoping for a while to establish a permanent office there. These California houses were inspired by the materials and spirit of the area and were built primarily of concrete.

Wright viewed concrete as an inexpensive, durable, and, most important, malleable building material without a personality of its own. His pursuit of its full potential began with Unity Temple in Oak Park, Illinois, in 1904 and continued with intermittent periods of obsession. Because concrete submits itself so willingly to whatever an architect desires, Wright sought ways to take advantage of its plasticity. The sunny California climate seemed the perfect place to do so.

After flirting with concrete ornament in the Hollyhock house in 1917, Wright designed four concrete textile block houses in the Los Angeles area between 1922 and 1926. Lloyd Wright, the architect's oldest son, actually supervised the construction of most of them after his father returned to the Midwest.

The houses recall Mayan and Japanese influences but relied heavily on American technology of the twentieth century. To create the decorative textile blocks, concrete was precast into hollow blocks on site by unskilled workers, using local rock and sand. Steel rods were then interwoven in the hollow chambers of the blocks, which were set with no mortar joints; instead, they were filled with grout or concrete to give them strength. Intended to be built inexpensively, the textile block houses proved quite the opposite. The blocks were not uniform and required tedious adaptation to lay evenly. Wright was busy in Japan and was not available to solve problems.

The geometric blocks nonetheless created striking patterns when laid up in walls. The result was cool edifices of contemporary forms, nestled into the hills overlooking Los Angeles. Their sandy texture and sculpted shapes rise like sand castles on a dune.

In Wright's Ennis house of 1923 in Los Angeles, stacked textile blocks create a colonnade through which the indoor and outdoor rooms reveal themselves. A golden Tiffany glass mosaic of wisteria glistens above the fireplace in the hallway. [Julius Shulman]

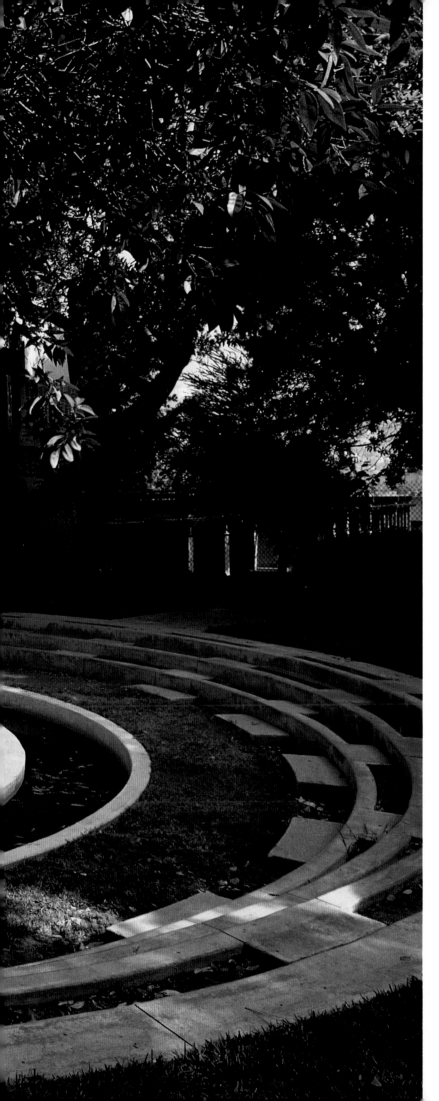

HOLLYHOCK HOUSE

High atop Hollywood's Olive Hill, Wright sculpted a home in 1917 for oil heiress and theater dévotée Aline Barnsdall. The architect responded to the barren site with a new interpretation of his organic architecture that marked the beginning of his California concrete era. Although planned for reinforced, poured concrete, it is mostly stucco on wood frame, but it still incorporates specially cast concrete ornament. The hollyhock flower, the client's favorite, was the inspiration for the abstracted decorative patterns in the concrete, art glass, and oak furniture.

Only one building of a planned performing arts complex, the house is oriented toward a center garden court and punctuated by several geometric pools. The design creates a private world where guests can freely circulate throughout the living spaces and gallery, into the gardens, and even up to the rooftop terraces for a longer view of the city.

Inside, the monochromatic, even surfaces come alive with color. The recently restored living room is another exercise in shades of gold and green. Custom oak furniture completes the inviting spaces, for which carpets also were designed. The incredibly complex, mirror-image table, lamp, and sofas that have been recreated draw guests around the central fireplace. Between the hearth and the sofas is a reflecting pool, a cooling contrast to the warm room. Over the fireplace, lattice grillework directs sunlight into the room like a theater spotlight on a star. Japanese decorative arts fit comfortably into the room, which was designed while Wright was working on the Imperial Hotel.

In 1927 Barnsdall donated the home and grounds to the city of Los Angeles, which continues to be responsible for its care and public access.

A circular pool highlights the central courtyard. Looking back at the house, a concrete passageway ornamented with stylized hollyhocks provides a compressed space that is released into the garden. The composition of geometric forms, like musical chords, creates a controlled architectural harmony. [Scot Zimmerman]

Following pages: The restoration of the living room included the recreation of the large sofa-table-lamp piece. It completes a unique setting focused on the fireplace, which is surrounded by a reflecting pool. Japanese screens are integral to the room's design and may have inspired the gold metallic paint on the walls. [© Alexander Vertikoff]

FREEMAN HOUSE

The concrete house that Wright created in Los Angeles in 1923 for Samuel and Harriet Freeman is, at 1,200 square feet, a compact and pure example of his textile block system of construction. The various geometric designs cast into the blocks create a texture that dominates the feel of the building. This tactile quality gives the cool concrete material an earthy appeal.

The dominant building material is also the dominant interior design element—yet another expression of Wright's quest for unity. The geometric masses that result from stacking these sixteen-inch-square blocks express the efficient, open spaces within the home. The square is most certainly the unit of design for the building. Some of the blocks are perforated to let light filter in through the pattern; others are solid, providing a counterpoint to the texture. Some are filled with glass to create windows; others are structurally supporting. Some are grouped to create a ceiling; others are widely spaced to provide doorways. Some are stacked thirty feet high; others reach out over the hill on terrace walls.

Approaching the house, only the closed side of the second story is visible. Yet variety and imagination are apparent. Entering through a compressed hallway, the living room explodes right in front. Light, shadows, and texture are everywhere. Wright conjured up a cool, protected place out of the sun's burning rays.

The furniture, which was not designed by Wright but by a one-time Wright apprentice and friend of the Freemans, Rudolph Schindler, is as unique as the building. The versatile upholstered and cabinet pieces capture the intimacy and simplicity of the spaces; some convert to various uses. Cool concrete meets warm wood tones and golden upholstery fabrics. Pottery, native American textiles, archaeological fragments, and wooden sculptures reinforce the primitive, cavelike feeling within the home. By day, the large glass expanse draws one to the light and the city below. But at night, the fireplace in the opposite wall beckons to the protected center, a place to reflect and share ideas. It is a refuge.

For sixty years, this house was a popular gathering place for artists, actors, dancers, and musicians. In 1983 Harriet Freeman donated it to the University of Southern California, whose care and study of the building are shedding new light on Wright's novel textile block design form.

1930s DESIGNS

The late 1920s and early 1930s were the most barren years of Wright's long career, in terms of the number of commissions. At age sixty-five, many men would have accepted this drought as a natural call to retirement. Not Wright. Never unchallenged, Wright-the-architect called on Wright-the-author and Wright-the-teacher to lead him out of financial hard times.

As a means of sorting out his life and promoting his self-proclaimed genius, Wright wrote *An Autobiography,* which was first published in 1932. This popular book, reprinted several times, inspired new interest in his work and consequently new clients. Soon afterward, he and his new wife, Olgivanna, founded the Taliesin Fellowship and began to build Taliesin West. Among the early apprentices there was Edgar J. Kaufmann, Jr., the twenty-four-year-old son of a wealthy Pittsburgh merchant. While he stayed at Taliesin for only a few months, Kaufmann, inspired by the autobiography and his experiences, introduced his father to the work of Wright, thus instigating a patronage that gave new life to the architect's career. Fallingwater, a revolutionary country house that Wright designed for the Kaufmanns, was without a doubt a powerful response to those espousing the new European International Style.

The other pivotal patron to appear in the 1930s was Herbert Johnson, president of the Johnson Wax Company. Wright's streamlined design for the firm's 1939 administration building in Racine, Wisconsin, with its lily-pad-like columns, confirmed that Wright's genius had not tired but had new energy. Wright was later asked to add a research tower to the building and design homes for Johnson and his daughter.

In these years of introspection, Wright created his two most celebrated works: Fallingwater and the Johnson Wax Administration Building. But there was plenty of time left to create his master plan for American cities, Broadacre City. The huge model, which the apprentices built, and the book and lectures he wrote about it were the subject of numerous assessments and diverse opinions. Interest blossomed in Wright's ideas. From 1935 to his death in 1959, Wright completed nearly two hundred more buildings.

At Fallingwater nooks and crannies permitted the Kaufmanns' fine sculpture collection to be dis-played. Uncharacteristically, Wright even left some limited wall space for paintings. [Christopher Little]

FALLINGWATER

In late 1934 Wright visited a waterfall near Mill Run, Pennsylvania, where Liliane and Edgar J. Kaufmann hoped to build a weekend retreat. Wright was moved by the beauty of its rock ledges, lush foliage, and rushing waters over Bear Run. The native vegetation, especially the rhododendron and mountain laurel, flourished in the moist shade. Sandstone boulders marked the prehistoric landscape that had been a favorite preserve for the Kaufmanns and their employees. When he received a detailed topographical map, Wright set about designing Fallingwater, which became the most renowned building of his career. Built into the side of the hill, and over—not across from—the picturesque waterfall, its design was a celebration of the site (pages 2–3). When it was completed in 1935, the Kaufmanns truly had a home where they could entertain their friends and commune with the wonders of nature. In 1963 Edgar Kaufmann, Jr., donated the house and 1,500 acres to the Western Pennsylvania Conservancy so that it would be protected and enjoyed by others.

Like a giant tree, Fallingwater grew from the site. The roots are the boulders on the valley floor. The trunk is a thirty-foot-tall layered sandstone chimney core. Its branches are low cantilevered terraces of reinforced concrete, the first-floor slab reaching eighteen feet beyond the stone piers. The rock ledges were the inspiration and became part of the composition: the four largest boulders are so integrated into the building's structure that the pivotal one is exposed in the living room as the hearth. The stream is so much a part of the house that a suspended stairway leads directly into it.

Edgar Kaufmann, Jr., described Fallingwater's relationship to the surrounding forest.

The materials of the structure blend with the colorings of the rocks and trees, while occasional accents are provided by bright furnishings, like the wildflowers or birds outside. The paths within the house, stairs and passages, meander without formality or urgency, and the house hardly has a main entrance; there are many ways in and out. Sociability and privacy are both available, as are the comforts of home and the adventures of the seasons. So people are cosseted into relaxing, into exploring the enjoyment of life refreshed in nature.

The living room, roughly 1,800 square feet of flexible space, is masterfully shaped into more intimate areas for dining and relaxing. Ceiling levels, lighting, masonry piers, and furniture groupings work together to focus attention on a certain spot, the waxed flagstone floor stretching beneath all. Upstairs, both master and guest bedrooms open to private terraces (pages 12–13). Each has its own fireplace. The third-floor study and gallery are connected to two more terraces and a tiny treetop nook.

From the highest balcony to the plunge pool beneath the living room terrace, the diverse spaces offer opportunities for privacy or sociability. The refinements of a cultured life are accentuated by the simplicity of the natural setting. At Fallingwater, Wright's imagination and coordination set new highs.

Opposite: From the colors of the sandstone, Wright selected a light chamois for the long, graceful stretches of concrete. His favorite color, Cherokee red, outlines the long bands of windows, creating a snappy, secondary rhythm. Terraces to the east and west served as viewing platforms and gathering places.

Above: The site's key boulder became the living room hearth.

Following pages: The furniture's simple, geometric shapes provide a background for patterns and textures of handcrafted fiber arts. Red remains the principal accent to the warm buffs and grays. [Photographs by Christopher Little]

WINGSPREAD

Just north of Racine, Wisconsin, Wright orchestrated another house totally at one with its site. Only a half mile from Lake Michigan, the spot now occupied by Wingspread was once a nature preserve. It is lush with mature pines, arborvitae, wooded areas, ponds, and lagoons. The house shares thirty acres with an abundance of waterfowl and wildlife.

Wright called Wingspread another Prairie Style house, because it was similar to the zoned plans of earlier commissions such as the Coonley house of 1908. However, it is a bolder, freer interpretation that is quite different from its older siblings and in many ways more like a Usonian. The house was created for Herbert F. Johnson, president of the Johnson Wax Company, shortly after Wright designed the company's noted administration building. Before the house was completed in 1939, Mrs. Johnson died. Johnson moved in nonetheless and continued to live in the spacious house for twenty years. It now serves as a conference center and the home of the Johnson Foundation.

Wingspread is built on a square grid, which is incised into the highly waxed, red concrete floors, and accented with powerful diagonal lines. At the center is a monumental, curvilinear fireplace core. Around this gracefully articulated central mass are all of the living and entertaining spaces. Each has its own fireplace. Wright called this thirty-foot-high area a wigwam. Shallow steps and ceiling heights define the shift from one area of the space to another. Wings spread out in four directions like a pinwheel. One is for the master bedroom suite, one for the children's bedrooms; another is the guest wing, and the fourth is the service area.

The craftsmanship is exemplary. The only ornament is the careful handling of the building materials themselves: flawless Cherokee red brick masses; great expanses of smooth, seemingly nail-less bands of oak veneer; perfectly cut sandstone slabs; and meticulously crafted furniture.

Despite the grandeur of the spaces, the power of the horizontal line dominates. The wooden light decks and tiers of clerestory windows join the deeply raked horizontal mortar joints to create a visual unity. The eye is drawn to the people level. There, clusters of simple, comfortable furniture invite visitors to enjoy the variety of indoor and outdoor spaces—at the fireplace, by the pool, in the library. A few well-selected works of art complement the spaces but do not detract from their simple elegance.

Opposite: The central core is a giant curved chimney. Warm brick and oak tones are enriched by abundant natural light from above and on all sides. The curved shapes of the chimney, the stairway to an observation point, and the barrel chairs add an undulating rhythm to the primarily square space. [Richard Cheek, Yale University Press]

USONIAN HOUSES

Shifts in American lifestyles and the need for economical housing challenged Wright throughout his career, particularly in the late 1930s and the 1940s when Wright observed changes in American families. Most of them owned automobiles; they were home less often; more women were working; most families had no servants; time spent in the kitchen was also family socialization time; life was more and more informal. Wright's solution was Usonian houses, a term he used to describe buildings uniquely suitable for life in the United States of North America (USONA). His concepts were a part of his larger vision for a decentralized Broadacre City.

Wright developed a pattern, a way of building, that would respond to these shifts in society. The kitchen was open to the dining area at the core of the house. Spacious living areas opened in one direction; bedrooms extended in the other direction and were small with many built-ins to conserve space. The homes usually had flat or shallow-pitched roofs and were one story. They stretched sensitively across their suburban lots, offering a private street side with few windows and an open garden side with generous terraces. Built on concrete slabs, the houses were heated by water pipes buried in the floor. Each house had a module, or unit system, that formed the basis for its construction; this unit was incised into the wet concrete floors and served as a grid on which the house was built. The square, rectangle, hexagon, and triangle took their turns as these modules.

One of the fundamental principles of Usonian architecture was that it should be affordable. Throughout his career Wright experimented with new ways of building to eliminate costly skilled craftspeople and expensive materials. He felt most challenged by clients who had big desires but a small pocketbook. He encouraged them to participate in the building themselves. Wright developed efficiencies in design that produced efficiencies in construction and lower costs, without compromising beauty— instead, reframing it. The methods were applied to small houses as well as to larger commissions and became the framework for his remaining designs.

Wright designed two houses for the Herbert Jacobses. Their first, in 1936, was his first Usonian. The second, built in Middleton, Wisconsin, in 1948, is a solar hemicycle tucked into an earthen berm on the cold north side. The curved southern wall seen here is open to solar rays that warm the house. [Ezra Stoller, © Esto]

HANNA HOUSE

Moved by Wright's philosophy of architecture, Jean and Paul Hanna, a young professor at Stanford University, approached Wright with their ideas and budget. His response was a magnificent design in Palo Alto, California, based on a hexagonal module, like a bee's honeycomb—thus giving the home its name, Honeycomb house. Wright opted for a 120-degree angle over his favored 90-degree angle, demonstrating yet another method of breaking out of boxlike rooms.

The house for Catherine and Herbert Jacobs, then under way in Madison, Wisconsin, established Wright's vision of a Usonian house. The 1936 house for the Hannas was a larger interpretation of the same concept, but its hexagonal module differed from the Jacobses' four-by-two-foot rectangle. Unfortunately, but not surprisingly for Wright, the house far exceeded the Hannas' modest budget. Somehow, it got built.

The house adapted easily to the changes in the family's needs for more than thirty-five years. During that time, they added a guest house and a hobby shop as well as a garden house. Their extensive landscaping enhanced the building's relationship to the gently sloping site. In 1974 the Hannas donated their beloved home to Stanford University. Before suffering extensive earthquake damage in 1989, it served as the home of the university's provost.

Wright's use of flexible, mostly movable, interior and exterior walls gives the home a Japanese feeling. Entire window walls swing open, allowing the living spaces to flow out onto the concrete terraces. It also permitted the couple to convert many of the spaces to new shapes and uses when the children left home. The vertical module of the redwood board-and-batten walls relates to the horizontal module. The rooms casually wrap around the contours of the site to form spaces that slowly reveal themselves. The hexagonal unit creates a natural gentleness in the meander of the spaces. The trellis-like windows frame garden views in all directions. The inner court with a cascading pool provides an embracing garden refuge.

Inside, the original furnishings repeat the hexagonal motif. Interesting patterns are created when right-angled brick joins at 120-degree angled corners. A tall fireplace reaches out of its pit and into the living room. Grass matting covers the ceiling and adds a natural texture next to the smooth wood surfaces. The home is breezy, sheltered, cool in the summer heat. Radiant-heated floors are partially covered with neutral-colored, simple-textured carpets.

In the Honeycomb house, obtuse angles seem to accept and respond to human activities more naturally than abrupt right angles. This is one of Wright's most welcoming interiors.

Following pages: The natural tones in the living room become a quiet backdrop for the exuberance of the meandering spaces. With its hexagonal module, the home has a compelling flow that carries the eye from room to room and inside to outside without interruption. These flexible, open spaces responded to the family's needs.

Opposite: The garden terrace floor continues the hexagonal module. Even the light seems to be cast in hexagonal patterns. As in Wright's other Usonian houses, terrace doors open out from the living room, inviting the patterns and colors of the magnificent garden into the house. [Photographs by Ezra Stoller, © Esto]

ROSENBAUM HOUSE

When Mildred and Stanley Rosenbaum were married in 1938, the groom's parents lured them back to Florence, Alabama, with the promise of an architect-designed home. Learning of Wright's work, the young couple eagerly sought his help. They became early pioneers of his Usonian concept of moderate-price housing for American families. Their 1,540-square-foot house, built in 1939 for $12,000, was one of Wright's finest.

Sensitively sited on two acres overlooking the Tennessee River, it is a simple horizontal statement. The cypress and brick home is based on a rectangular module and is placed on a concrete slab with heating beneath it. All walls and windows are aligned with a grid that is incised into the floor. The L-shaped plan is typically private on the street side and open at the back. Behind the entry, at the core of the house, is an open kitchen and dining area, which Wright called the workspace. One wing provides three bedrooms and two baths. The other includes an ample living room and library. A later courtyard addition, also designed by Wright, increased the bedroom area needed for the family's four sons and changed the plan to a T shape.

All rooms open freely to the outdoors through floor-to-ceiling doors and windows, borrowing space, light, and color from nature. Rows and rows of multicolored books line the walls.

Clerestory windows with perforated panels bring light into the closed side of the house. While many pieces of built-in and free-standing furniture were designed for the home using the same two-by-four-foot module, as well as the same cypress, the owners felt free to restructure the various components and to select other furniture. Charles Eames's molded plywood chairs and rectilinear upholstered pieces are compatible with the Wright tables and cabinets. Mildred Rosenbaum's favorite color, teal blue, complements the warm tones of the board-and batten walls.

For fifty years, the home has successfully responded to the changing needs of the original family. The playground has become a Japanese garden. A bunk room has become a weaving studio. And now it is open to the public by appointment.

Above: Like other Usonians, the Rosenbaum house is strongly horizontal. The front is private with few windows, but the back opens to the surrounding landscape from nearly every room. French doors welcome sunlight into the spaces. [Courtesy Mildred Rosenbaum]

Opposite: The dining area, built into an area that is offset from the living room, opens to the kitchen on the left. Plywood chairs by Charles Eames blend naturally with the built-in cypress furniture designed by Wright. [© Yukio Futagawa]

Opposite: Modular plywood furniture was grouped into various configurations as needed. Throughout, a neutral gray offsets the dominant Cherokee red. Cutouts in the clerestory panels, characteristic of the Usonian houses, repeat the geometric theme of the house, while they filter light and frame treetop views.

Above: A view of the modest house at dusk shows how the cypress boards have weathered to gray. Openings in the roof over the windows keep the light shining through despite the broad overhangs. The entrance portecochère is at right, the private terrace on the left. [Photographs by Ping Amranand]

POPE-LEIGHEY HOUSE

"Will you create a house for us? Will you?" newspaperman Loren Pope wrote to Wright in 1939.

There are certain things a man wants during life, and, of life. Material things and things of the spirit. The writer has one fervent wish that includes both. It is for a house created by you. Created is the proper word. Many another architect might be able to plan or design a house. But only you can create one that will become for us a home.

Two weeks later came the reply from Wright: "Of course I am ready to give you a house."

Simply built of cypress boards sandwiched over a plywood core, brick, and glass on a concrete pad, the house that Wright gave to Loren and Charlotte Pope in Falls Church, Virginia, eliminated all that was not essential. Another of Wright's L-shaped Usonian plans, built around a large tulip poplar tree, the 1941 house was a modest 1,200 square feet. Its flexibility meant that less space was needed. The ornament came from the materials themselves: the placement of windows, wood joinery and cutouts, patterns of the masonry. Simple linen and jute mats in a biscuit color covered the red floors.

The living and dining areas are a few steps down from the entry level, so that the changing planes define activities, create interest, and adapt the building to its site. A sanctum or study is to the right of the entry. Opening to the outside on two sides, the house is filled with light and changing shadows all day. Despite the simplicity of the economical two-bedroom home, it is visually stimulating in every direction. The component seating and table groups can be gathered into various compositions for dining, conversation, lounging, or bridge parties. Again, Wright designed for efficiency and flexibility as well as aesthetics. One naturally followed the other.

The Popes sold their house to Marjorie and Robert Leighey in 1946. After living there for eighteen years, the Leigheys learned that a planned interstate highway was destined to go right through their living room. Rather than see it demolished, Marjorie Leighey donated the house to the National Trust for Historic Preservation. It was then dismantled, relocated, and rebuilt on the grounds of another National Trust property, the early nineteenth-century Woodlawn Plantation, in Mount Vernon, Virginia—a study in residential contrasts. While house moving is not the best way to save a building, it may, in some cases, be the only way.

WALTER HOUSE

After selling his road-building company in 1944, Lowell Walter sought to build a retirement home. Rather than move to Florida or California, he selected a site on a family farm in Quasqueton, Iowa, where his family had lived for generations. Walter wanted an architect who would be sensitive to the beauties of the Midwest. What Wright produced the following year was a complex of buildings, including the house, a two-story river pavilion, and an outdoor hearth called "council fires," all suited to the informal lifestyle of the countryside. The eleven-acre site is now operated by the Iowa Department of Natural Resources, to which Walter bequeathed it in 1981.

One enters the estate through Wright-designed iron gates, down a drive lined with evergreens of many varieties, including local cedars. Only low shrubberies were planted near the house itself, creating a soft mat for its base. Gradually, the house, called Cedar Rock, is approached across a terrace, past flower planters. Sited on a hill overlooking a bend in the Wapsipinicon River, the house is built of red brick and based on a square five-foot, three-inch module. Massive masonry walls lift the home above the hillside, create delicate grilles, and define indoor and outdoor spaces. The roof is reinforced concrete, cantilevering out beyond the walls but pierced over the windows.

The living room, or garden room, is actually a rotated square projecting out from the bedroom wing like a flower on a stem. Waxed walnut boards run the length of the gallery and are used in the shelves, defining the room's shape. Pieces of the beautifully crafted walnut furniture can be fitted together in various arrangements. The curved edges, either concave or convex, like that of the wood moldings, repeat the curve of the roof edge. A fireplace, large enough to accommodate five-foot logs, rises from its shallow pit. Tropical plants hang from planters above the soffit and fill planters built into the red concrete floor. The ceiling is pierced with square skylights to nourish the interior gardens. The walls are glass on three sides, mitered at the corners, and mirrored on the fourth. The room is an open garden pavilion with only a roof for shelter.

The living room overlooks the ambling Wapsipinicon River. Generous windows and a pierced roof flood the room with enough light for an interior garden. Smooth lines in the fine walnut cabinetry create elegance in this country setting. [Ezra Stoller, © Esto]

ZIMMERMAN HOUSE

Dr. Isadore Zimmerman and his wife, Lucille, a nurse, were one of many of Wright's clients who were drawn to his work through his autobiography. They were delighted with the opportunity to let Wright transform their personal interests and lifestyle into a concrete statement that suited their site. In that they allowed Wright a free rein and also shared his love of music, they were ideal clients. Isadore Zimmerman was an accomplished violinist who also studied and played the piano, and Lucille played the piano and cello.

While considered a Usonian design because of its chronological age and construction style, the Zimmerman house, built in Manchester, New Hampshire, in 1950, recalls Wright's earlier Prairie Style period as well. Its concept was economical, but the execution was more extravagant because of the selection of materials and the owners' demand for first-class craftsmanship.

The broad, sheltering, gently sloped roof and horizontal profile nestle the home quietly into its wooded lot. Although Wright specified wood shingles, red clay tiles were ultimately used on the roof but have since been replaced with asphalt. The street elevation is private, with only a strip of special perforated concrete blocks framing small windows above the red brick base. This combination of materials was new for Wright. Specially beveled, carefully selected cypress boards were screwed into place, then the hole was plugged, making it invisible. A four-foot-square grid was incised into the concrete floor, but the vertical unit used throughout the house was thirteen inches.

The garden room, the main living area, doubled as a concert space for the Zimmermans' friends, who gathered to share their love of music. The quartet stand is based on the one used at Taliesin. The southwest exposure opens to a beautifully landscaped garden abundant with rhododendron and punctuated with oak, pine, ash, and maple trees. Golden light fills the space on cold winter evenings. Five brick piers, with glass between, create a structural rhythm. Planters extend from one side of the glass to the other, blurring the distinction between inside and out. The other rooms are small to accommodate the generous living room within the limits of the 1,458 square feet of the entire house.

A high-back bench, chairs, and hassocks are upholstered in handwoven fabrics, selected by Wright, in golds and rusts. A six-panel Japanese screen is attached to the end wall. Lamps have Japanese paper inserts. Over the years, the Zimmermans became avid art collectors. While they could not display paintings, their home became a personal gallery for their collection of three-dimensional art. They were especially fond of the pottery of Edwin Scheier but also collected sculpture by others.

Consequently, they developed a close relationship with the Currier Gallery of Art. On Lucille Zimmerman's death in 1988, her home was bequeathed to the gallery, which has undertaken its restoration and provides guided tours.

Above: The living room gains its perceived size by annexing the adjoining terrace. Planters line the glass, which seems to dissolve the definition between inside and outside just as the mitered corner window does. The private wooded site became a part of daily life within the home. [Photographs by Ezra Stoller, © Esto]

Opposite: The garden room seems spacious despite the house's modest size. Behind the brick fireplace are the workspace and the bedrooms. Scored with the module of the house, the waxed, red concrete floor covers radiant heating coils. The furniture is economical and flexible as well as a freestanding architectural element.

LIVING WITH WRIGHT

LIVING WITH WRIGHT'S EXTRAORDINARILY INTEGRATED VISION OF WHAT A HOUSE SHOULD BE POSES REAL CHALLENGES. WHAT CAN CHANGE? WHAT SHOULD STAY THE SAME? MANY PRIVATE OWNERS HAVE MET THIS CHALLENGE WITH RESPECT—AND SOME PATIENCE.

Opposite: Mary and William Palmer have successfully faced the challenges of living in their Wright home in Ann Arbor, Michigan, for forty years. Fortunately, their personal interests in gardening, Japanese culture, and music are in sympathy with their exquisite Usonian house. The waxed red floor, incised with a triangular module like the house itself, serves as a glowing backdrop for the autumnal colors of the living area. The room is a large triangle that projects into a woodland garden that the Palmers have created and nurtured for many years, embracing the Wrightian spirit with which their house was designed in 1952. [Balthazar Korab]

THE CHALLENGE

The vast majority of Wright's residences, 269, are still privately owned by individuals or families. They are not museums. They are lived in by people who may have growing children, or hobbies, or pets. And living in a house designed by a world-renowned architect presents some difficult choices when one wants to update or adapt to new life patterns. The inherent public responsibility of owning such a house is, one hopes, repaid by the daily rewards of living in the harmonious environments that Wright created.

Reflected Marjorie Leighey about the Pope-Leighey house:

At first there is quiet pleasure and thankfulness for being surrounded by something so admirable to look upon. Then comes the business of living. . . . Comes a time of rebellion, an anger at any dwelling-place that presumes to dictate how its occupants live. . . . Comes the time for decision. Do we truly like the house? Would we rather live here than anywhere else? Again the beauty spoke. . . . Intelligence was put to work to see how to live within the now-accepted limitations.

Private owners like Marjorie Leighey, especially those who are not the original clients, have had to determine how their homes can best respond to their needs and their tastes and yet not upset the integrity of Wright's masterful spaces. Some have indiscriminately altered their buildings, tragically ignoring the original design intent and leaving great challenges for future preservationists. Others have carefully and sensitively made alterations. Some of these changes have been restorations, reversing inappropriate renovations.

Still other homeowners have not made architectural changes but have, for one reason or another, furnished their homes, at least partially, with items that were not specifically designed for them but that are perfectly compatible. These owners have been able to respond to the powerful expectations of Wright's legacy without sacrificing their own individuality. In fact, each is enhanced.

The owners of the homes shown here are representative of many who have successfully personalized their Wright houses. They have often gone to extraordinary lengths to do so and are to be commended for their investment in America's architectural heritage.

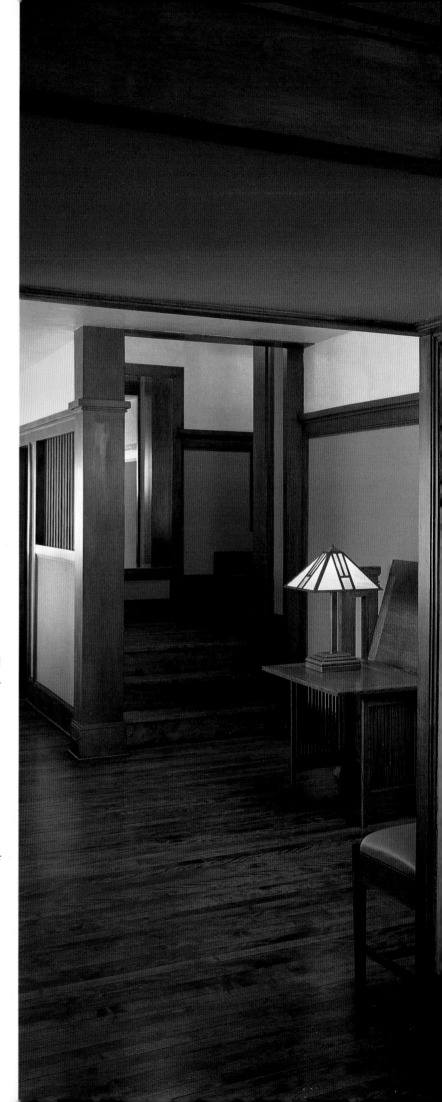

The current owners of the Henderson house have carefully furnished their early Prairie house with appropriate period items. The print table in the entrance hall is like ones on which Wright displayed his favorite Japanese woodblock prints. [© Judith Bromley]

HENDERON HOUE

One of the earliest Prairie Style designs, the F. B. Henderson home in Elmhurst, Illinois, is often compared to the Hickox house built the previous year, 1900, in Kankakee. The similar floor plans include an elongated octagon that is shared by the living room, dining room, and library. The hipped roof and ribbons of art glass windows beneath broad sheltering eaves clearly reflect Wright's style of the decade. The space flows freely through the house, which is anchored by a broad, central chimney. The subtle design of the brickwork gives an illusion of a concave arch over the hearth, drawing one to the center.

The current owners compare their home to a city loft space because of the openness of the first floor. A myriad of white and clear windows in simple compositions of squares and rectangles further extend the rooms into the garden and adjoining veranda. Original colors have been returned to the walls. The characteristic autumnal scheme has pumpkin walls below, with a stippled, light maize color above the russet-stained birch wood banding.

Lacking information about the original furnishings, the family has sought reproductions of other Prairie Style and Arts and Crafts furniture. Some are custom designs; others were mass-produced. They blend smoothly and compatibly with the architecture of the rooms. The caramel leather seat covering of the settle, which is a reproduction of a Wright design for the Greene house in Aurora, Illinois, draws its color from the brick. A Stickley rocker echoes the rectilinear forms. The oak dining room furniture, recently custom made, was inspired by similar designs for the William Martin house in Oak Park and the Barton house in Buffalo. The octagonal posts of the chairs and table base repeat the octagonal bay in which they rest. Beneath, Oriental and Turkish carpets in geometric designs tie together groupings of furniture within the larger spaces.

When family members turned their attention to renovating the landscape, they sought to complement the rigidity of the house's geometry with a natural, prairie garden. The undulating curves of the garden beds lead to protected play areas and quiet places to rest. Perennials, trees, and shrubs, particularly ones native to the midwestern prairie, were selected to provide a continuously changing display of colors and textures throughout the seasons. The bone stucco walls, trimmed with brown and capped with a cedar-shingled roof, provide a neutral background for the magnificent natural forms from which the house was born.

BOYNTON HOUSE

It is curious that a house built for a widower and his teenage daughter would have such generous dining and kitchen facilities. A cook and a maid also lived in the home, but it is not known if the businessman, Edward E. Boynton, or in future years his married daughter, were avid entertainers. Wright beautifully articulated and carefully supervised the construction in 1908 of this classic Prairie Style home in Rochester, New York. So, it is assumed that the attention he paid to the food preparation and serving areas was a reflection of the client's interest.

The spacious dining room has two tables. The larger one has low lamp columns near each corner that also serve as flower holders. Not as high or obtrusive as those on the tables of the Robie or May houses, they focus the diners' attention on the intimacy of the table gathering. The smaller table near the expansive window bay overlooks the garden and would have been perfect for the two Boyntons dining alone. The room is further highlighted by art glass—covered ceiling lights and a band of clerestory windows over the light screen on the south wall. The dominant motif in the plentiful art glass is the square.

The kitchen retains the original, simple pine cabinets, which have been restored by the current owners. A wood-color laminate now covers the counter tops, replacing the original wood, but the center island is still topped with hard maple. A commercial range and a restaurant rack above the island are practical additions. The maple floor, covered with linoleum by a previous owner, has been restored. Storage space is augmented by an adjoining pantry, now a gallery for the owners' handmade pottery collection, as well as a huge basement pantry. Baskets and other pieces of favorite art collected at art fairs around the country add to the personality of the home.

The two principal bedroom suites clearly respond to the desires of the two original occupants. The master suite has simple built-in cabinets but minimal closets in the dressing room. It is spacious yet simply appointed, perfect for a man. Young Beulah's rooms, on the other hand, have generous closets and built-in cabinets in the dressing room, ample space for many dresses and gowns. Mirrors around the dressing table fold open for a complete viewing.

The care and spirit with which the Boynton house was built are matched by the attention of the conscientious current owners.

Above: The pantry provided storage and a preparation area for this home designed for entertaining. The new owners' pottery collection and Oriental carpet add unusual interest to what was once just a simple serving area.

Opposite: The kitchen of the Boynton house is essentially original. Only small modifications have been made to update the turn-of-the-century room. The oak cabinets and the center island have new laminate tops, and a restaurant rack has been added for storage. Track lighting focuses light on various work spaces.

Following pages: The expansive dining room is a spectacular stage for entertaining. The larger of two tables is beneath a low ceiling and framed art glass lights. Clerestory panels shed light onto the table, which has its own built-in light columns. The other table, in a higher space within an elaborate art glass bay, is surrounded by the garden view. A linear band wraps around the entire room to provide the needed human scale for an intimate gathering. The owners' art and carpet collection complements the simplicity of the three-dimensional geometric forms. New wall sconces maintain the square detail of the room. [Photographs by Andy Olenick, Fotowerks]

INGALLS HOUSE

The projecting porch, cantilevered balconies, and simple, stucco surfaces of this 1909 house in River Forest, Illinois, are reminiscent of the house Wright designed for Elizabeth Gale in Oak Park the same year. However, the symmetry and formality of the street facade are somewhat unusual for Wright. Even the art glass window designs are symmetrical, a bow of triangles above a rectangle with a low hipped roof like the house's own profile. Resting far back on its generous suburban lot, the house appears tranquil.

First-floor spaces radiate from a central Roman brick fireplace, with smooth oak moldings linking and defining the various planes. Upstairs, four bedrooms and one bathroom surround the central hall. It was a simple but compact plan that fulfilled the desire of the clients, Mr. and Mrs. J. Kibben Ingalls, for maximum ventilation.

But the present owners wished to stretch out and increase their living area as their family needs grew. The tiny, outdated kitchen was a particular concern. Inspired by Wright's own symmetry, they saw an opportunity to expand the home without altering the primary spaces or the street facade. They nearly mirrored the east elevation on the west side. Additions to Wright's buildings, usually discouraged, require courage as well as a total understanding of and respect for the original design intention. The result here is a unified plan that enhances rather than diminishes the house's harmony.

The original kitchen and a 1926 porch addition by Wright apprentice William Drummond were removed, and a large, modern kitchen–family room was added. Matching Wright's plan for the front of the house, the back includes a terrace with a cantilevered roof. A bit more width was achieved by making the north and south bays added on the west slightly larger than those on the east . The new informal cooking and gathering space nearly doubles in size in warmer months when activities reach out onto the terrace overlooking the garden. Upstairs, a small bedroom was enlarged, and a ribbon of windows replaced the single original one. In total, twenty-one new art glass windows and doors were fabricated to match the originals.

All of the changes were carefully documented, leaving a complete historical record. Every detail, every molding, every finish, and, most important, the scale and open plan are in keeping with Wright's grammar for the house.

Opposite top: The addition to the back of the house mirrors the front elevation and repeats all of the elements so sensitively that the home, while altered, is enhanced—a challenge for any owner of a historic house. The deck extends beyond the enlarged kitchen area and adds additional space in warm weather.

Opposite bottom: A spacious new kitchen replaced a tiny outdated one. Appliances are hidden behind oak doors, including a slatted screen for the microwave. Moldings continue detailing used throughout the house, maintaining the flow of space. Dinner is served on a china design from Wright's Imperial Hotel. [Photographs © Steve Grubman]

COONLEY PLAYHOUSE

When their glorious, pavilioned estate, the Coonley house, was completed in 1908, Mr. and Mrs. Avery Coonley were so energized that they decided to build a school in Riverside, Illinois, to further their ideals of progressive education. In 1912 Wright produced a cubist composition reminiscent of a Froebel block construction from his childhood. Dozens of colorful art glass windows, inspired by the balloons, flags, and confetti of parades, lined the walls. Their bright primary colors and lively geometric designs make them some of Wright's most famous windows. Sadly, the building served as a primary school only for a few years. Over the next sixty years, it was remodeled extensively, and most of the windows were sold.

Energetic new owners have thoughtfully restored the Coonley playhouse, including meticulously reproducing most of the windows using photographs and existing examples as their guide. While the open plan serves their needs as a home, it is also a splendid gallery space for their extraordinary collection of decorative arts. Fused glass is displayed in and on Arts and Crafts cabinets, illuminated by light from the three tall front windows. Ribbons of clerestory windows allow treetop views but no distractions.

In the other direction, one is drawn to the fireplace, three steps up on a stage. Nearby, chairs and tables designed by noted furniture designer George Nakashima work as components much like Wright's Usonian furniture. They can be regrouped easily for different purposes. All are constructed of walnut to match the extensive millwork in the room. Handwoven fabrics, some with colorful, geometric designs inspired by the windows and subtle grillework patterns, cover the seat cushions and stools.

Following pages: To avoid blocking the view of the hearth yet provide seating there, the owners commissioned Nakashima to create a piece that would solve this dilemma and match chairs of his they already owned. The Roman brick and plaster walls provide a neutral background for sculpture and other art. [Chester Brummel]

Recapturing the original schoolroom feeling of the front of the house, the owners have surrounded not just one but several Stickley tables with chairs. While these serve as pedestals for artworks, they also function as work or dining tables, perfect for large dinner parties. [© Judith Bromley]

BOGK HOUSE

Born in 1916 while Wright was immersed in the construction of the Imperial Hotel, this town house in Milwaukee was an artistic amalgam of various inspirational sources. It was built for the family of F. C. Bogk, a civic leader and banker. Whether seen as a transitional design or as a unique statement of its own, the house is unquestionably successful. A low hipped roof shelters the richly ornamented brick cube. Like a treasure box, it holds many jewels.

The living room, one and a half stories high, bestows its magical gifts. Originally painted metallic gold with a celadon-colored ceiling, it has a distinct Oriental flavor. Fortunately, the clients shared Wright's fascination with Japanese art. George Niedecken, Wright's able associate in Milwaukee, coordinated the interiors. Small squares of golden glass sparkle in the windows. More small squares march around the edges of the cabinetry, adding to the rhythm. Multiple custom carpets with medallions composed of squares in a variety of sizes and colors were designed to unify the spaces and confirm the color scheme. Attached and free-standing furniture expresses the grammar of the Prairie School but has a subtle Japanese feeling.

Walnut moldings wrap the walls, leading the eye from one interesting space to the next. Passing a fish pond, one is drawn up three stairs, beyond a planter with lanterns in a garden alcove, to the dining room. A wall of vertical art glass windows opens the room to the garden. At the center is another version of Wright's well-known straight-back chairs and rectangular table. These pieces, however, are partially caned, a unique and possibly Japanese variation. Custom light fixtures and a buffet complete the unified environment.

In the early 1960s the current owners commissioned Wright's followers at Taliesin to refresh the home's interiors. The soft earthen color scheme was changed to jewel tones of turquoise, carnelian, and citron. Carpets were rewoven in the original patterns but in the new colors; the originals were given to a museum. Furniture that remained has been augmented with pieces Wright designed for the Heritage-Henredon Furniture Company in the 1950s and with others designed by the Taliesin architects. New upholstery fabrics were selected. The house became a brighter version of its former self.

Vertical lighting fixtures are recessed into the walls, offering diffused light through art glass panels and repeating the verticality of the tall windows and masonry piers. [Eric Oxendorf]

STORER HOUSE

John Storer's 1923 house in Hollywood became the manifestation of Wright's newest synthesis of experiences and influences—a textile block house. Built for a retired doctor, the house encountered innumerable problems during construction, as did the other textile block houses. The cost overruns were enormous. Sadly, Storer died, bankrupt, in 1927. His dream home passed from hand to hand until 1984, when it was purchased by a film producer, who has now completed a comprehensive restoration enhanced by his own collections.

In a most unusual plan, two bedrooms are on the first floor, and others are above them on the main floor along with the dining room and kitchen, which open onto garden terraces. The living room rests immediately above the dining room, on the top floor, like a watch tower, with verandas for scanning vistas. Columns of glass and textile blocks rise two stories on both sides of the living-dining core.

Four geometric block designs are rhythmically intermixed in vertical and horizontal patterns, forming solid walls, windows, grilles, fireplaces, terraces, and pools. They sculpt imaginative and mysterious indoor and outdoor rooms from the earth.

The home is furnished with an extraordinary collection of Wright and Arts and Crafts decorative objects. Because no furniture was custom designed, the owner has blended pieces made for other Wright buildings: a Prairie Style chair comfortably shares space with a Usonian chair, related by their rectilinear origins. Designed in the center of Wright's career, the house seems to serve as a bridge between his various furniture styles now seen within its walls.

While generally faithful to the original plan, the owner and his architect, Eric Lloyd Wright, grandson of Wright, made two sensitive changes. They added a swimming pool, edged in matching textile blocks, that fits neatly into the back of the tight hillside lot. A modern kitchen also was installed without disturbing the historic architecture but deriving its forms and inspiration from it.

Following pages: The living room now doubles as a retrospective exhibition of Wright's designs, supplemented with other compatible classic works. [Oberto Gili, *House & Garden.* © 1990]

Textile blocks line the entrance terrace, with its refreshing pool. The house's landscaping, designed by Wright's son Lloyd, softens the edges of the blocks and naturally emphasizes various elements. [© Yukio Futagawa]

AULDBRASS

Wright was soon given an opportunity to apply his Usonian concepts to a southern plantation. The result was a rambling, informal complex of residential and farm buildings in Yemassee, South Carolina, that was far from the formality of the traditional southern mansion. The Leigh Stevens family occupied Auldbrass plantation beginning in 1939 and owned the home for more than thirty years.

Based on a hexagonal module, thirty inches on a side, the spaces take on an undulating openness. Wright reacted to the ubiquitous live oak trees and the sway of the Spanish moss by adopting their angle for the house's walls. All of the walls thus are sloped inward nine degrees, as well as from left to right—certainly creating a complex composition of angles to challenge the masons and carpenters. An abstracted version of moss is the basis for the downspout designs that fall from the corners. The pattern in the glass doors recalls a live oak branch. Tidewater cypress planks form the walls around the radiant-heated Cherokee red slab floor. Overhead, 33,000 square feet of new pleated copper roof shelters all.

As in antebellum days, the kitchen was placed in a separate building connected to the main house by an open pergola, which isolated the cooking heat; the connecting space has now been enclosed, creating a long dining room between the areas. A modular table of three five-foot hexagons, two parallelograms, and three triangles can be arranged in a variety of patterns suitable for up to eighteen guests. A breakfast room overlooks the pool. Cool breezes are invited in through dozens of french doors opening to terraces on all sides.

The complexity of this angular puzzle continues. Perforated screens above are cut in diagonal patterns inspired by the Yemassee Indians, creating a shadow stencil for the light. Only a few pieces of the cypress plywood furniture that Wright designed still remain in the home. They have been restored, and dozens of new pieces were constructed from original designs, all of which are based on a hexagonal unit. Triangular hassocks (partial hexagons) are clustered in various patterns; benches, shelving, and counter tops wrap around hexagonal walls; chair legs angle out beyond chair backs; hexagonal beds have adjoining triangular tables. Textured upholstery fabrics and soft blue-greens complement the warm tones of the wood, brick, leather, and colored floor. Despite the complexity, the abiding feeling is tranquility.

Wright was called back to make modifications in 1951, but the years that followed took their toll on the property. In 1987 it was rescued by a new owner, who has worked diligently to recapture the original spirit. Since then, all of the buildings, furnishings, and grounds have been meticulously restored. Auldbrass is again a collector's hospitable retreat that provides an alternative to our right-angled world.

Opposite top: The complex composition of angles in the house begins with the nine-degree inward slope of the walls, which mirrors the slant of the surrounding live oak trees. Numerous 60- and 120-degree angles are created by the hexagonal module on which the house is built.

Opposite bottom: The dining area was created from the passageway between the kitchen and the main house. Various component tables and chairs are clustered to take advantage of the view of the pool and the garden. The setting is informal and relaxed and at one with the site.

Following pages: Carefully selected accessories enrich the living area. Stuffed wild animals, watching from walls and ledges, pay homage to Auldbrass's years of service as a hunting lodge. Angular Arts and Crafts lamps, ceramics, and copper carry on the theme. [Photographs © Yukio Futagawa]

BROWN HOUSE

In designs for several cooperative residential subdivisions, Wright combined his interest in affordable housing with his ideas for community planning. One such project was the 1947 plan for Parkwyn Village in Kalamazoo, Michigan, which laid out dozens of circular lots around a small lake. The common area between the circles was planted with native vegetation.

In 1949 Eric and Ann Brown built one of four Wright-designed homes that were completed on a gracefully flowing street. Like the others, it was constructed of specially designed blocks of cast concrete, a readily available and economical material in the postwar era. Using a square module, the house extended 135 feet to include five bedrooms for the couple's three children, father-in-law, and housekeeper, but it still maintained the intended benefits of simplicity. The shallow-pitched roof with a fine gravel cover nearly blends into the gravel driveway, presenting a sheltering entrance.

The fireplace—with its surrounding pool, a dramatic feature of the spacious living room—has a six-foot-wide opening to accommodate extra-large logs. All rooms but one face the southwest to maximize the sun's warmth in this northern climate. A complementary color scheme arose from the architect's desire to use gold and the client's fondness for blue-green. Brightly colored pillows, nubby textured fabrics, and ceilings of Honduran mahogany bring additional warmth into the cool gray rooms.

For four decades the home has successfully adapted to the changing needs of the family. Ann Brown's interest in the arts was considered in the early plans and continues to be served by the spaces. The living room converts to a concert hall when the two pianos are surrounded by the numerous modular seating pieces. The fine acoustics needed for her piano classes also manage to protect the bedrooms from excessive noise. The children's bunk room has recently become her painting studio. And the desire for space in which to exhibit her work and their collection of paintings found a creative solution: wide shelves were placed along one of the few plain walls, and paintings are stacked several deep on each. Those visible on top are rotated to provide a personal gallery with any number of changing exhibitions.

The simple, neutral concrete surfaces serve as a canvas for the family, their activities, and their art.

Opposite: One of the challenges of living in a Wright house is finding wall space for paintings. Ann Brown devised a set of shelves near the entrance to hold her collection of paintings. Those on top are changed whenever desired. With its surrounding pool, the fireplace is the focus of the living room. [Balthazar Korab]

LOVNESS STUDIO

In his Usonian period, Wright was particularly challenged by prospective clients who approached him with overwhelming enthusiasm but a small budget. Such was the case with Donald and Virginia Lovness of Stillwater, Minnesota. Wright encouraged them to undertake a "do-it-yourself" house to save money, as he did with many other clients in the postwar years.

The house that had been estimated at $83,000 cost them only $20,000 in 1955—plus, of course, a treasury of personal commitment and two years of back-breaking effort. Originally conceived as a Usonian Automatic, Wright's experimental system using specially cast concrete blocks, the design evolved into a stone structure at the owners' insistence. Stone by stone, the young Lovnesses built their home according to Wright's design.

What they call their studio is a compact plan based on a simple four-foot-square module. Dolomite masonry piers support a cantilevered flat roof above a concrete slab floor. The open side of the house has floor-to-ceiling doors and windows, mitered at the corners, welcoming nature inside. Light is drawn into the house's closed side through square clerestory windows in the workspace. The geometric elements overlap and interrelate with each other and with the stone columns and decks of the building itself, creating a multidimensional sculpture. Donald Lovness, an accomplished woodworker, has continued to build, including numerous pieces of oak furniture designed by Wright for their home; Virginia Lovness does the finishing and upholstery. Together, architect and clients created a home with the richness and serenity of a temple.

Situated on a wooded hill above a small semiprivate lake, the house is a restful, artful retreat. Its low profile, not visible from the street, emerges at the end of a narrow drive with a pond on one side and a lake on the other. The 26,000 pine trees planted on the former pasture land have matured into a surrounding forest.

In 1972, after four years of work, one of four cottages that Wright designed for their lakefront was completed. Nestled into its lot, the cottage contributes to the harmony of the setting, repeating many of the house's elements and sharing the beauty of the site.

The Lovnesses built more furniture for their three-level cottage, including a table and chairs in the dining area based on other Wright furniture designs. [Photographs © Norman McGrath]

The house's dining table and chairs, built by the owners, create a rhythmic composition as they unite with the shelving unit that separates the workspace from the dining area. A layered light fixture of squares and rectangles is suspended above. Red is again used as an accent to the natural tones of the wood and stone.

The Lovness studio has a simple plan yet an elegance that stems from the spirit of the architect-client relationship. The personal interests of the owners are reflected here—their meticulous woodworking and passion for Asian art are at one with the simplicity of the architecture.

PALMER HOUSE

Wright often attracted clients who shared his interests as much as they liked his architecture. They hoped that their home would be more than a shelter from the elements, just a place to sleep and eat—that it would be a life-enriching environment. They were rewarded with homes that nourished their interests and their spirits.

When Mary Palmer, a graduate in music theory, visited her first Wright home, she later wrote, "His architecture is like a Beethoven quartet. It is vibrant. It is exciting. It is harmonious." She related to Wright's ability to compose a building. Together, Mary and William Palmer worked with Wright to create a new opus that has become more beautiful every year.

A triangular module was the basis for their home in Ann Arbor, which was built in 1952 on a protected hillside near the University of Michigan, where William Palmer taught economics. Entering from the carport, one gradually ascends a dozen broad, shallow stairs in a long, open corridor of russet brick with bands of perforated ceramic blocks, their pattern reflecting the house's floor plan. To the left, toward the light, the space of the living area bursts forth. Straight ahead, a narrow passageway leads to the bedroom wing, located in a second triangle.

The primary room is a large triangle that projects dramatically into a meticulously landscaped garden. Clear-grained, red tidewater cypress boards rise to the ceiling above. Ambers, mossy greens, and rusts, inspired by the tones of the cypress boards, have been used for upholstery fabrics and cushions. Handwoven throws, scarves, and Japanese textiles add counterpoints. A delicate pattern covers, then hangs, like an obi, from the backs of the dining chairs, softening the edges of the cypress. Down several shallow stairs, broad eaves provide shelter to the terrace, an extension of the indoor space.

The Palmers' interest in gardening and Japanese culture intensified in their new home. Japanese floral arrangements inside lead the eye beyond, to a garden that has been gradually, naturally, evolving for four decades.

In the living room, triangles and parallelograms form as the furniture and house merge. By day, the waxed red floor reflects light from the windows. At night, indirect lighting in decks casts a golden glow as it reflects off the cypress ceiling. [Balthazar Korab]

Opposite: The Palmers were moved by restful pauses in the temple gardens they visited in Japan and sought to establish that experience in their own garden. Working with former Wright associate John Howe, in 1964 they built a triangular garden house that repeats the module and style of the main house. [Balthazar Korab]

Above: While the house looks outward, the garden house in the Palmers' hillside looks inward, a deliberate spiritual metaphor. Simple Japanese floral arrangements focus attention on particular architectural details in this intimate, sunken, and carefully controlled space. The garden itself was developed by the Palmers to reflect

Wrightian principles. To the original white pine and hardwoods have been added more pines, English yews, holly, leucothoe, ferns, bleeding hearts, and a profusion of euonymus. Thousands of bulbs begin each season's pageantry. Native woodland flowers are clustered along the shady, bark-covered paths that meander along the hill-

side. An informal water course with a pool reflects and cools as it moves the eye through the garden. The garden house is a destination in itself or a stop during a walk along the garden path. [© Judith Bromley]

THE WRIGHT INFLUENCE

WRIGHT INSPIRED SEVERAL GENERATIONS OF ARCHITECTS. FOR SEVENTY YEARS, HE TAUGHT ORGANIC ARCHITECTURE, AND YOUNG ARCHITECTS LISTENED. THOSE COMMITTED TO HIS DEEPLY HELD PRINCIPLES CONTINUE TO RESIST FASHIONS AND PROVIDE UNIQUE AMERICAN DESIGNS.

Opposite: The Fisher house in Sisters, Oregon, designed by former Wright apprentice Milton Stricker, was created a century after Wright designed his first home in Oak Park and is located 2,000 miles away. Yet the principles underlying each are the same. The house created for the Fishers is a reflection of the uniqueness of the occupants; it embraces its site; it uses natural materials, some taken from the surrounding area; it is centered on a warming hearth; it draws its colors from a natural palette. It is a unity of color and form. [Randy Shelton, Architectural Images]

WRIGHT'S ASSOCIATES

Frank Lloyd Wright's contribution to American architecture did not end with his death in 1959. It is alive and well. He directly inspired hundreds of apprentices who worked at his side in his Oak Park studio and, later, at the two Taliesins. The Taliesin Fellowship, which began accepting students in 1932, provided a hands-on apprenticeship in designing, building, and artful living. Some stayed for only a few weeks, others for decades, a few for a lifetime. Many carried Wright's principles with them as they established their own practices and developed their own admirers. With Taliesin Architects, Ltd., a for-profit subsidiary of the Frank Lloyd Wright Foundation, the fellowship continues to teach through practical experience.

Wright taught principles, not a style to be slavishly imitated. The degree to which the former associates have individualized their interpretation of those principles of organic architecture varies greatly. Some of the early draftsmen in the Oak Park studio deviated little from Wright's actual Prairie Style designs. In fact, their buildings are often mistaken for his. Wright depended on his architects to be extensions of his hand—as he was a "pencil" in Louis Sullivan's hand—to produce thousands of drawings and make on-site decisions. This expectation of fidelity became a privilege and a burden.

In contrast, some who studied with Wright in the later years at Taliesin, such as John Lautner, have strongly resisted being categorized as practicing a Wright style, despite Wright's profound impact. "Architecture in its truest sense," said Lautner, "may not be academically defined. If it is, it becomes a dead, non-growing entity or cliché." The majority of the former apprentices still practicing today would no doubt agree. Countless other architects never worked in Wright's studio but had parallel careers or studied his work thoughtfully from afar. It would be futile to estimate the impact of this one man on the architecture profession during the past century—as well as on all of us whose perceptions of architecture have been irrevocably changed.

The houses that follow are a small sample of the work of some of those whose response to the needs of their clients was based on their experience with Frank Lloyd Wright.

Wright with his Taliesin Fellowship in 1937. In the top row, the second, third, and fourth from the left are John Lautner, John Howe, and Gene Masselink. In the bottom row, second from right, is Wesley Peters. [Hedrich-Blessing, Chicago Historical Society]

BARR HOUSE

During the twelve active years of Wright's Oak Park studio, some two dozen draftsmen and one woman moved in and out through its doors. Many came for only a few weeks to work on a project; others were more steady assistants. Among the latter was William Drummond, who came to Wright in 1899 and stayed for most of the next decade. On leaving Wright's studio, not long before Wright himself left to go to Europe in 1909, Drummond established himself as a less troublesome alternative to Wright. Many opportunities came his way from past and potential Wright clients, Mrs. Avery Coonley among them. He was particularly well received in River Forest, where he completed sixteen commissions, including his own home next door to his coworker Isabel Roberts.

This stucco, board-and-batten house designed for librarian Charles Barr in River Forest in 1912 was a typical commission. Although it was prepared during his three-year partnership with Louis Guenzel, it is distinctly from Drummond's hand. The indirect side entrance is gracefully sheltered and defined by the landscaping and a small projecting wall. The crisp, clean-edged lines and angles are characteristic of his version of the Prairie Style. The horizontal emphasis in the bands of art glass windows, shallow hipped roof, wide overhangs, and simple geometric forms are similar to those from Wright's office. Drummond was adept at the grammar of the Prairie Style, borrowing from Wright without actually copying him.

The differences are most apparent inside. A bold fireplace mass anchors the house at its center and opens on three sides to the living room, dining room, and hallway. The living room gives way to a projecting front porch and adjoins the dining room in a compact but seemingly spacious plan. The simple lines and neutral color of the owners' furniture permit an uninterrupted appreciation of the architectural elements. The geometric compositions drawn by the intersection of lines and planes are defined by extensive wood moldings and decks. This bright, open interior is an efficient manipulation of a forty-foot-square plan into interesting and adaptable spaces.

A later addition on the back of the house has recently been reworked so that it is more in keeping with the original designs and proportions. The roof pitch, cantilever, and art glass windows now echo the original elements.

Below: The Barr house illustrates how Prairie Style elements were used by other architects. The low sheltering roof with broad overhangs, light screens alternating with solid screens, a horizontal emphasis, and a geometric simplicity are features recognizable in many midwestern communities. Here, the board-and-batten walls draw the home closer to the site, underscoring with their horizontal lines the unity of the elements. [Photographs © Steve Grubman]

Opposite top: The living room's light, neutral color scheme assures that its geometry has no competition. Classic Breuer chairs and a marble dining table contribute their simple shapes.

Opposite bottom: A kitchen renovation maintained the original space but organized it differently, keeping the scale, the flow, and the linear quality. New cabinets match the house's woodwork; familiar wood moldings unite openings.

PURCELL-CUTTS HOUSE

William Gray Purcell grew up not far from Wright's studio in Oak Park but never actually worked there. He did, however, work for Wright's teacher, Louis Sullivan, for a few months in 1903; there, he met George Grant Elmslie, who served as chief draftsman for nearly twenty years. After forming a partnership in Minneapolis in 1907, Purcell and Elmslie became the most prolific of the Prairie School architects, continuing to design in the style after World War I.

Composed for Purcell's own family in 1913, this house in Minneapolis was one of their finest. In 1985 the Anson Cutts family, which had owned it for sixty-six years, bequeathed it to the Minneapolis Institute of Arts, which has undertaken a thorough restoration and opened it to the public.

Elmslie brought a hand well schooled in interior ornamentation to the partnership. The fluid, nature-inspired art glass, stencils, murals, furniture, and carpet designs in their projects were largely his work. Purcell's genius was evident in the layout of their houses. They, too, sought an American architecture that responded to the openness and flexibility of its lifestyle and natural beauty. While it is hard to calculate Wright's influence on their work, Sullivan's inspiration is an undeniable common thread linking them.

A variety of spaces in the long, narrow stucco house are found on several levels. A vaulted ceiling spans the ground-level living room and the second-level dining room before it gives way to the projecting terrace ceiling. Beneath are finely detailed and sometimes whimsical components that all neatly interrelate. A tiny writing nook in a corner of the living room provides a personal space with its own desk. But the fireplace wall was given the greatest attention. The naturalist and the craftsman worked together in wood and brick, paint and glass to accentuate the quiet power of the horizontal line. A triangle motif is repeated in all of the art glass and in some of the furniture. Stencil designs ring the ceiling, some resurrecting the triangle theme. Even the globes of the lights are sponge-painted to blend with the mottled rosy sand walls.

The varied, integral ornament and the extraordinary craftsmanship enhance the function and warmth of the home. The feeling is mellow and unified but more delicate than Wright's interiors.

Opposite, top left: The delicate art glass windows that open up the entire house came from the hand of George Elmslie. These corner examples use the geometric motifs so common in Wright's own designs. As double triangles, the diamonds continue the triangular theme that unites the entire house.

Opposite, top right: Seen from the stencil-lined upstairs hall, the bedroom at left has a compact children's bed, built in like much of Wright's furniture. Oriental rugs add a touch of red to the soft natural tones of both bedrooms, highlighted by the wood paneling and floors. [Photographs by C. M. Korab, Balthazar Korab Ltd.]

Opposite, bottom left and right: Wright's collaborator Richard Bock contributed the sculpture, *Nils and His Goose,* that perches on the angular storage cabinet between the living and dining rooms. At the writing nook tucked into a corner are a triangular-back chair and a perfectly framed view of a wildflower garden.

Following pages: Charles Livingston Bull's mural of blue herons rises over the fireplace like the moon within its design. The soft mauves, gray, and rose tones set the color palette for the space. Iridescent Tiffany glass glistens in the horizontal joints of the masonry. The oak trim even has a lavender filler beneath its waxed finish.

ERSKINE HOUSE

John S. Van Bergen, an Oak Park native, was one of the last to join Wright's Oak Park studio. He arrived in early 1909 after apprenticing for two years with Walter Burley Griffin, another Wright protégé. Van Bergen also was the last to leave, staying on until 1911 with Isabel Roberts to complete the work that Wright had abandoned when he went to Europe in 1909. After opening his own office in Oak Park, Van Bergen continued to design Prairie Style houses until they went out of fashion during World War I. He is credited with eighteen houses in Oak Park alone between 1912 and 1926, most of them Prairie. Van Bergen was so extremely faithful to the language Wright devised that little of his own creativity is apparent in many of his works. After the war, a return to more traditional styles left most designers who had been seeking a new American architecture scrambling for work. Van Bergen moved to Chicago's north shore, where he designed many interesting houses, and eventually went to California, where he practiced until he was eighty years old.

Van Bergen drew heavily on Wright's design for a "Fireproof House for $5,000," which was published in the *Ladies' Home Journal* in 1906. Later, he borrowed ideas from the American System Built Homes that Wright designed for the Richards Company in Milwaukee. The 1913 house in Oak Park built for lawyer Robert Erskine and his family was typical of Van Bergen's versions of the "Fireproof House." Intended to be poured concrete, it was stucco on wood frame instead. Its compact, thirty-foot-square plan fits neatly on the urban grid for which it was designed. Beneath a low hipped roof are a living room, dining room, and kitchen on the first floor and three bedrooms and a bathroom on the second. An early addition included a first-floor den and bathroom and an extra bedroom to the rear.

No space is wasted. It is efficient and economical yet offers many of the distinctive features of larger Prairie Style houses. A sheltering porch provides a welcome at the side entrance, easing the transition inside. Van Bergen varied the plan by placing the entrance between the living and dining areas rather than between the kitchen and living room. A large, rectilinear fireplace marks the center of the house, with bands of art glass windows defining the perimeters. The wood stripping on the exterior and interior walls emphasizes the rectangular forms that are repeated throughout. Leading the eye horizontally from one space to another, they attempt to destroy the box as much as possible, giving the illusion of much grander spaces.

Opposite top: The current owners have found a suitable setting for their extensive collection of Arts and Crafts furniture and ceramics. Selected pieces of Mission oak furniture, including Stickley items, have been purchased at auctions and from antiques dealers. Newly designed dining room furniture, inspired by the Robie house chairs, was integrated into the room.

Opposite bottom: Arts and Crafts pottery, so popular when the home was built, fills the shelves with geometric shapes and colorful glazes. Most were made by Marblehead, but Teco, Grueby, and Rookwood also are represented. The cool greens and blues are a perfect accent to the golden Prairie interior. [Photographs by Chester Brummel]

SCHINDLER HOUSE

One of the few apprentices who worked with Wright during the transition between the Oak Park studio and the Taliesin Fellowship was Viennese architect Rudolph M. Schindler. Schindler and his wife, Pauline, were inspired by Taliesin's unified experience of work and play in a natural setting. In 1920 Schindler went to Los Angeles to supervise the Barnsdall projects for Wright, but by 1921 he had established his own practice. Its base until his death in 1953 was this innovative home and studio in West Hollywood.

Designed and built that first year jointly by the Schindlers and their close friends, Clyde and Marian Chase, the complex incorporates some distinct Wright influences as well as new poured-concrete technologies with which Chase was familiar. Like Wright's buildings, it is based on a unit system organized into flexible, inspiring spaces and is intimately related to its site. While the use of walls of doors that open to outside gardens is similar to Wright's treatment of the Hollyhock house, many of the Schindler house's techniques predate applications by Wright in his later Usonian designs.

The most radical departure from traditional plans was the owners' scheme for cooperative living. As Schindler described it:

The basic idea was to give each person his own room—instead of the usual distribution—and to do most of the cooking right at the table—making it more a social "campfire" affair, than the disagreeable burden to one member of the family. . . . Each room represents a variation on one structural and architectural theme. . . . the basic requirement for a camper's shelter: a protected back, an open front, a fireplace and a roof.

Open-air sleeping was accommodated by a rooftop porch, and a guest wing was included to provide rental income.

The house is built of durable and easy-to-maintain concrete and has a gravel roof. Employing what Schindler called his slab-tilt system, the forms were constructed horizontally; then the concrete was poured, finished, and left to dry, following which the slabs were tilted into vertical positions with a block and tackle. The spaces left when the forms were removed were filled with concrete or glass.

The couples built their own furniture over several years, then the Chases left in 1924 and were replaced by the family of Richard Neutra, another Viennese architect who also had worked briefly with Wright. For a long time, this communal home typified the creative, progressive ideologies discussed within its walls.

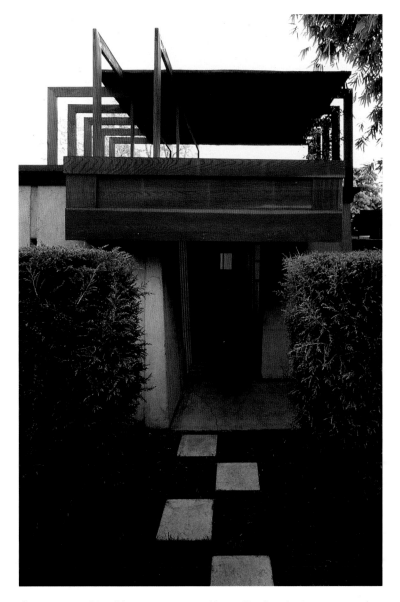

Opposite top: Movable partitions and patio walls are simple screens of wood with glass or Insulite.

Opposite bottom: Patios and sunken gardens create extended and defined outdoor living areas adjoining each room, with outdoor fireplaces reinforcing the concept of an actual living room.

Above: Bamboo hedges protect the privacy of the 100-by-200-foot site, which since 1980 has been owned by the Friends of the Schindler House. The cool gray of the concrete is complemented by redwood tones used in posts and ceilings. Copper fireplace hoods pick up the color inside. [Photographs © Grant Mudford]

DOW STUDIO

Early in life, Alden Dow, son of the founder of the Dow Chemical Company, demonstrated a fondness for and a sensitivity to design. In fact, he was drawn to architecture when he stayed at Wright's Imperial Hotel as a child, visiting Japan with his parents. Like Wright, he dabbled in photography as a means of recording the images of life in a composed format. Soon after graduation from Columbia University's school of architecture, he and his wife, Vada, spent a memorable five months at Taliesin in 1933. There, Dow found someone who shared his interest in nature, in the relationship of a building's materials to its design, and in the impact of a building on its occupants—a kindred spirit.

He soon opened his own studio in Midland, Michigan, where he practiced architecture until his death in 1983. Dow named his design philosophy "composed order." It recognized, he explained, "that there may be many good answers put together in a variety of ways and that truly great results come from an organic or growable idea on which smaller contributions can develop. The ideal is to achieve harmony among the people, materials and ideas involved." He was so admired for his contribution to his home state that he was named its architect laureate in 1983. The Alden B. Dow Creativity Center was founded to perpetuate his commitment to quality and innovation.

Like Wright, Dow focused his career on residential architecture. Over the years he designed sixty homes in Midland and many others elsewhere in the country. During the 1930s he built thirteen houses using a patented system called Unit Blocks. Among them was his own home and studio in Midland, built between 1937 and 1940.

There is no better example of his philosophy or his ability to intermingle nature and architecture than this inspiring composition.

The one-foot-square Unit Blocks were cast from recycled cinders from the Dow Chemical Company. He used them not only to form walls and terraces beneath the broad copper roof; they also took their place ornamentally in the surrounding pond, like stepping stones. Water is often an integral part of Dow's designs. Here, the pond he created stops just short of his studio, separated only by two layers of blocks. A conference room in the reception area, often called the submarine room, is actually two feet below the pond's surface. When the suns reflects off the water into the room, it dances on the walls. The porch and other rooms overlook the pond. Interior spaces flow quietly into the garden. There is hardly a pause where one meets the other.

Custom built-in furniture and other decorative arts that were designed or selected for the rooms maintain the geometry and the rhythm of the building. Modular stools can be pulled out from beneath multilevel tables to provide extra seating. Woven plastic strips conceal lighting in the living room ceiling. Unlike Wright, Dow used generous amounts of bright colors. Vibrant, clear hues contrast with white-painted cinder blocks throughout the complex, creating an excitement that challenges the serenity of the gracious spaces. The bright green carpet in one living room area yields to red in the next. Multicolored cushions dot the sofa. In Dow's office, multiple planes overlap in the ceiling, each another pure color—red, green, hot pink, purple, yellow. As Dow urged, "Separate parts put together so each part contributes the most to the others."

Opposite: Overlooking the pond, the living room of Alden Dow's studio is a rainbow of color. Painted cinder blocks provide a multidimensional backdrop for the splashes of gold, red, pink, and green. Dow was much more aggressive and experimental with his use of color than Wright. [Photographs by Balthazar Korab]

Dow shared Wright's love of red and appreciation for the simplicity of Japanese design, a fact that is evident in interior details as well as in the landscaping. This bridge shows his masterful ability to integrate fabricated elements with the natural. His use of a red linear design against the greenery is reminiscent of the gates at Taliesin.

The home and studio gradually takes form beyond the pond, its Unit Blocks gathered together beneath a low, angular roof. The integration of building and site is complete. Sixty-seven acres of magnificently landscaped gardens surround Dow's home and have evolved over nearly a century. Guests are welcome to amble through the botanical park, which offers with the change of each season new insights into the cooperation between nature and architecture.

BOWLER HOUSE

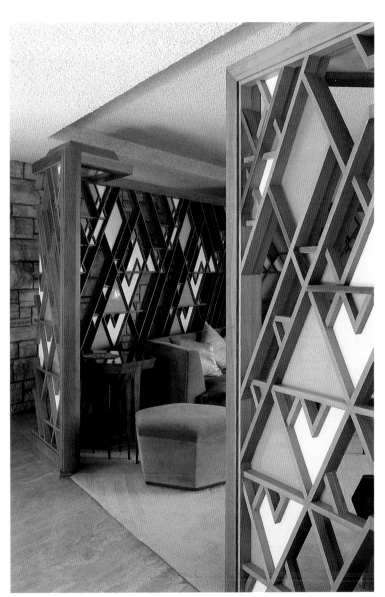

Lloyd Wright, actually Frank Lloyd Wright, Jr., the oldest child of the Oak Park family, was born the year in which Catherine and Frank moved into their home, 1889. As a young man he traveled to Italy to help his father prepare the drawings for the famous German publication of Wright's work produced by Ernst Wasmuth in 1910–1911. He was trained as a landscape architect in the office of the noted landscape architects Olmsted and Olmsted and later worked for Irving Gill, a California architect who did pioneering work in concrete technology.

From 1920 to 1925, while his father was traveling back and forth to Japan and later to the Midwest, Lloyd Wright supervised most of the California concrete block commissions then under construction, a project that proved frustrating given the elder Wright's inaccessibility. However, Lloyd Wright continued to experiment with concrete construction throughout the 1920s. His designs were often richly ornamented and imaginative, well suited to his California clientele. He practiced architecture and landscape design in the Los Angeles area until his death in 1978. His most well-known commission was the Wayfarers Chapel of 1951 in Palos Verdes.

John Bowler, a contractor for industrial buildings, had heard of Lloyd Wright through another client. Bowler needed a large family home for his four growing boys in Palos Verdes. In 1963 Lloyd Wright produced a fanciful form, somewhat like an exotic bird that has just landed on a rock ledge. Its reinforced concrete deck and slab, together with the wood-frame and stucco walls, establish a solid base for the complex plan, which is based on a diamond module. An unusual roof system of built-up roofing on a wood frame, with a thin layer of pumice concrete on top to protect it, has proven to be durable while maintaining the uniform texture of the walls.

Lloyd Wright, of course, beautifully landscaped the entire site and designed all of the furniture for the living and dining rooms. Velveteen upholstery on the seating pieces repeats the yellow-green tones of a geometric-patterned screen in the living room. Angles continue throughout the home. Mirrors in the bathroom are faceted like a crystal. The fireplace and rhythmic columns are a tan Arizona sandstone. The travertine floor was a later, but compatible, addition.

In the Bowler house, the architect was given the opportunity and freedom to create a total unity, inside and out, providing a durable and inspiring home base for the venturesome family.

Opposite: The tan color and aggregate texture of the Bowler house confirm its close relationship to the earth. Grooved industrial plastic "plummage," however, soars beyond the roof, its blue color blending with the California sky. The decorated geometric parapet rail on the first-floor deck is reinforced concrete.

Above: An elaborate screen in the living room, partially attached to the wall, is loosely based on an abstraction of a bird of paradise. Diamond and triangular shapes were formed by walnut strips filled in with anodized aluminum and plastic in gold, mossy green, and white. [Photographs by Alan Weintraub]

HOWE HOUSE

For twenty-seven years John Howe worked at the side of Frank Lloyd
Wright, directing the activities of his drafting room and completing
many of Wright's presentation drawings. As one of the first members
of the Taliesin Fellowship, he was well schooled in the principles of
organic architecture. After Wright's death, he established a successful
practice in Minneapolis, where, like Wright, he has focused on houses.

John and Lu Howe's own 1971 home, Sankaku, the Japanese
term for an equilateral triangle, is nestled in a hillside overlooking a
small wooded lake in Burnsville. The triangle gives the home not just
its name but also its energy and repose. The approach to the con-
cealed front door is down a naturally landscaped path, onto a deck,
across a bridge. Inside, a narrow hallway leads at an angle to open,
multilevel spaces that embrace their natural setting. Down a few
stairs, the living, dining, and kitchen areas open to the lake view.
Porches enhance the rooms spatially and aesthetically, drawing one's
vision and activities beyond the walls. The two bedrooms are on the
entry level, and a sanctum—like a treehouse—rests among the
branches at the top. Half walls are used when full-height walls are not
needed, opening the spaces one to another.

While compact, the house feels spacious because it bor-
rows space, visually, from outside and is not compartmentalized.
Soft light reflecting from light decks adds to the serenity of the living
room. The triangle reappears like an old friend in light fixtures, art
glass, furniture, stairway treads, and porches. It is reformulated into
hexagons for tables and cutout designs in the light deck.

All of the furniture was designed by Howe, but it bears a
close resemblance to familiar Wright designs. The long bench, triangular lounge chairs, and straight dining chairs all are scaled perfectly
to suit their purpose and their space. The gold and tangerine upholstery is a nubby, basket weave in contrast to the hard, clean lines and
smooth Philippine mahogany surfaces. Carefully selected accessories
project a love for fine craftsmanship and a respect for the artisan.
Simple Japanese art draws attention to a wall or a shelf. The
efficiency of the spaces is so enhanced by the personal interests of
the owners that the house radiates an inherent glow of harmony.

Like so many of Wright's own
houses, here the fireplace is at the
core, reaching for the roof. The
distinctively Wrightian table lamps
are modeled on a Taliesin design.
[Les Turnau]

GERINGER HOUSE

Arthur Dyson apprenticed with architects Bruce Goff and William Gray Purcell as well as Frank Lloyd Wright. From them he extracted a personal style that enables him to create original spaces from the unique needs and characters of his clients. Like Wright, the dry inventory of clients' needs is not as important as knowing what gives them pleasure, what aspects of nature they admire, and what the attributes of their site are. "Architecture is a philosophy towards life," he says, "an avenue which originates with living individuals and their requirements—incorporating everything from the pragmatism of resisting the elements to the poetry of ideals and dreams, and undertakes to provide a setting to awaken senses, to stimulate imagination and to expand consciousness in a world in harmony with its environment."

When asked to design a house in Kerman, California, for Ralph and Nancy Geringer, Dyson, now based in Fresno, found that this young farming couple with two sons wanted a home that would separate them from the fields of grapes that dominated their days. They desired a private shelter, horizontal and rustic in feeling, that would give them visual access to the views but protect them from the sun and wind and farm activities.

What they got, in 1979, was a farmhouse-in-the-round. The circular home, raised above the land, makes room for a lush oasis in its center court. A swimming pool, spa, and generous plantings on surrounding terraces contrast with the dusty fields outside their walls. All division walls radiate from the center.

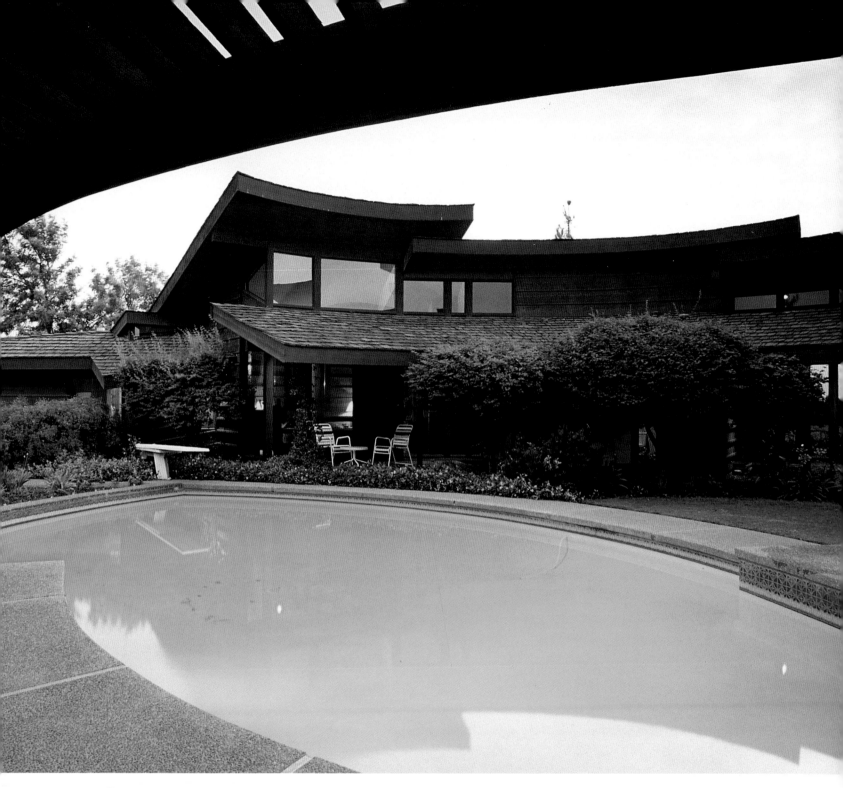

The kitchen opens to the game room and overlooks the pool. An overhead trellis holds pots and pans and repeats the trellises that are used elsewhere to filter light and link areas. Generous windows open the home to the center, offering terraces for indoor-outdoor living. Interior spaces are varied, some with high, soaring ceilings, others with low, intimate ones. Hidden corners throughout the house offer special views. Light streams through clerestory windows but allows privacy. The trellises and low roofs intensify movement in some areas, while others, such as the living rooms, emerge as open pools of space. The board-and-batten walls and cedar-shingled roof create interesting compositions as they curve and turn and shelter from the sun.

Opposite: An aerial view of the Geringer residence reveals the uniqueness of the site. Carved out of the flat surrounding fields, it is a private refuge, an innovative response to a farming family's needs.

Above: The round plan includes an interior garden court, pool, and spa. All rooms open to this pleasant oasis. The gentle curves and open but varied spaces within the home break the monotony of the row-after-row panorama of the family's daily work. [Photographs by Scot Zimmerman]

EDMONDƧON HOUƧE

The short time E. Fay Jones spent at Taliesin in 1953 left an indelible imprint on his life's work. As an apprentice who was a graduate of Rice University's architecture school, he quickly absorbed Wright's principles of organic architecture; they have guided his work into breathtaking directions. He has inspired emerging architects at the University of Arkansas for nearly forty years. His understanding of nature's systems and materials, his ability to translate them into forms responding to a client's needs, and his meticulous attention to detail have produced an abundance of award-winning buildings and the Gold Medal of the American Institute of Architects for himself.

The house Jones designed in 1979 for Don and Ellen Edmondson in Forest City, Arkansas, not far from the architect's office in Fayetteville, came about from careful analysis of the clients' desires and the potential of the dramatic site. The mutual trust among clients, architect, and an able builder produced a magnificent house that rises four levels within the trees on Crowley's Ridge, high above a lake.

Gracefully rooted to its site, the house is layered into the hillside like the dogwood that surrounds it. Broad horizontal tile roofs anchor the building, while creamy stucco walls and rich redwood details reach for the treetops. The clients preferred a more tailored look than stone would have given. They chose stucco, which offers a canvas for patterns cast by branches and leaves—using the trees to provide natural ornamentation.

Jones, with his associate on the house, Maurice Jennings, designed the outdoor sculptures, furniture, lamps, pottery, table linens, and even stationery so that the experience of living in the home would be harmonious. An E-shaped motif emerged from the structural elements and became an abstract pattern that reappears in various places such as the clerestory windows and the intricate trellis that connects the house to the guest house, a recent addition.

The living room is actually a series of indoor and outdoor spaces including a screened porch and a large deck. Ceiling levels reach up two stories, then drop down over more intimate areas. Accents of color—red, orange, blue—dot all of the rooms in pillows and cushions, like wildflowers in a meadow. Mirrors echo the natural light and subtle details, multiplying their effect. In the same way, the house serves as a mirror, echoing the fundamental geometry and simplicity of nature.

Opposite: On the fourth level of the house is the study, overlooking the bedroom above the living area. The neutral palette of the furnishings and the walls spotlights the detail and fine craftsmanship of the wood trim, which is redwood, while the cabinetry is a clear-finished red oak.

Above: The house is entered, gradually, at the second level, by passing through a gate, then through a courtyard and over a bridge. The varied planes, the seductive spaces, and nature's arms seem to point the way. The challenges of the steep site were well rewarded. [Photographs by R. Greg Hursley]

SEGEL HOUSE

Since studying with Wright for six years at Taliesin, John Lautner has earned international acclaim for his individualized architectural solutions. According to Lautner, the purpose of architecture is to improve human life, not to promote a particular style. He points to Gottfried Semper's "Four Elements of Architecture": the moral and spiritual element; the roof; the enclosure; the mound or foundation. From them Lautner creates sculptural forms for living. Based in Los Angeles for the past fifty years, his designs—often exciting engineering feats as well as artistic compositions—are concentrated on the West Coast.

Gil and Joanne Segel, a dance therapist, wanted something soaring, yet of the ground. It was to be solid and free, built of wood. Joanne Segel's collaboration with the architect yielded an undulating beach cave of wood, glass, and stone. The cooperation between client and architect is apparent in the unity of this design in Malibu, California, completed in 1979.

The orientation is up and down the beach, not a flat, panoramic view out to sea like many of its neighbors. The sweep of the sandy beach on one side, seen through an uninterrupted curved wall of glass, and the private garden on the other lift the spirit while rooting it to the earth. The three-inch edges of Douglas fir timbers that form the partially hyperbolic-shaped roof create a rhythm in the ceiling of the living room that appears to radiate from the round, poured-concrete fireplace at the corner. Boulders rising from the rock floor are mimicked by the soft irregular forms of the sofas the owner had fabricated. Natural cottons and linens in light creams and beiges provide the neutrality desired—because nature provides so many colors through the windows. The motor court adjoining the living room is designed so that when the cars are removed, it becomes a stone-floored entertainment area.

Upstairs, the dance studio is a celebration of curves accentuated by light patterns from trellised ceiling panels. Walls of concrete, which was used for soundproofing, have been covered with wood.

Every room has a view of the ocean. To improve the bedroom view, the roof of the living room was covered with green grass, concealing the roofing material. It is no wonder that Lautner refers to his practice as "mostly private homes hidden from sight."

Opposite top: The hyperbolic curve of the roof matches the rolling curves of the hills and rocks of Malibu's beach. Inside and out, the home is an extension of the landscape that is visible from its rooms. [Julius Shulman]

Below: The lush marble shower area combines natural tones of red on the outside and brown within. Wood paneling and rock forms that surround it create the quiet feeling of a private waterfall in a secluded forest. [Alan Weintraub]

Following pages: The contours of the house and the boulders outside it are repeated in the living room space and the shapes within it. Views looking toward the ocean to the left or the private garden to the right are framed by the walls and become decorative elements. [Julius Shulman]

Opposite, bottom left and right: Curves continue the motif of the house, from a black pool off the deck to a bar area surrounding a fireplace. The ocean's reflection in the glass further underscores the house's relationship to its site. [Alan Weintraub]

BENTON HOUSE

A community of architects who apprenticed with Wright until his death in 1959 continues to practice organic architecture, under the name Taliesin Architects, Ltd., from bases in Wisconsin and Arizona. Organized as a subsidiary of the Frank Lloyd Wright Foundation, they carry on the tradition of teaching while working. Over the past thirty years Taliesin Architects has completed hundreds of projects scattered throughout the world. William Wesley Peters, the first Taliesin apprentice, served as the senior architect until his death in 1991. He also was the designer for the finely composed Benton house in Malibu, California, begun in 1981.

John Benton was a long-time friend of the Wright family when he commissioned a new home for his wife, Melinda, and family that also had to accommodate their extensive collection of American art. Their five-acre, sloping site ends abruptly at a bluff overlooking the Pacific Ocean, projecting out beyond the adjoining land.

The architect's response was an L-shaped plan that placed all living spaces—the living–dining room, the study, and four bedrooms—parallel to the cliff edge, offering free views of the beach and the ocean to the south. Perpendicular to this sixty-foot wing is the service area, which includes a garage, entry, kitchen, maid's room, and office. Long, broad stairs drop slowly toward the cliff edge on one side. A curved terrace projects over the ledge on the other side.

Although based on a sixteen-inch grid (used alternately with a four-foot variation), the design is marked by a forceful triangular motif that is articulated in the pitch and jagged edges of the roof, garden shapes, lights, window and door mullions, and projections at either end of the plan. A third shape, a circle, creates garden motifs, a pool at the entrance, a terrace wall, and the roof tiles. The interplay of geometric shapes is skillfully composed.

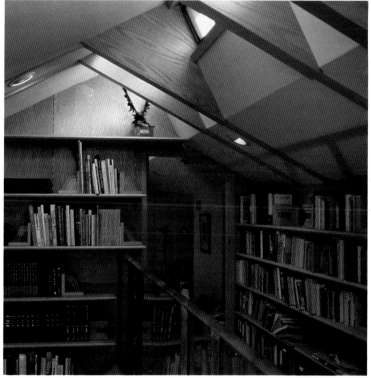

Top: In the dining and other areas, floor-to-ceiling glass walls open the home to generous terraces and a lush landscape. Caramel leather furniture and natural red oak tones in tables and cabinets harmonize with the warm color of the plaster. Scores of native American baskets rest on the horizontal decks that span the rooms.

Right: The clients' immense library was taken into consideration when the architets developed the plan for the house. Colorful ribbons of books lining the walls became striking decorative elements. There to be enjoyed, the books are easily found and read in the well-lit area. [Photographs by Taliesin Architects, Ltd.]

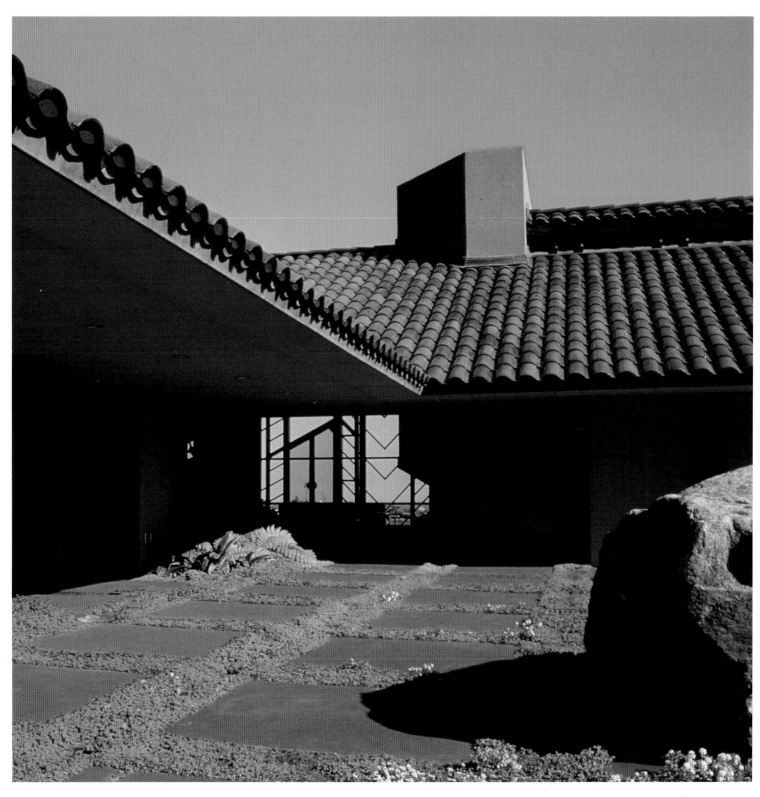

Above: Red squares in the courtyard are a reminder of the house's
module. Vertigris copper coating
on the window frames echoes the
deep green color of the ocean.
Combined with the cobalt blue
roof, the palette of the exterior is
decidedly more polychromatic
than the subtle interior.

Following pages: The blue of the
tile roof, the house's dominant
design element, exaggerates the
bright blue of the California sky
and rolls like the ocean. The muted
peach plaster that covers the
concrete-block and wood walls is
drawn from the tone of the land
and is a complementary back-

ground inside for Navajo rugs and
carefully placed drawings and
prints. Construction of the house
was a five-year project directed by
John Benton. The meticulous execution of every detail, including
custom-fabricated frames surrounding 641 window panes, yards
of cabinetry, installation of 276

built-in light fixtures, ceiling
marking strips, and light decks, was
all coordinated and supervised by
the owner himself.

FIJHER HOUJE

Originally from Wright's native Wisconsin, Milton Stricker joined the Taliesin Fellowship in 1952 after studying architecture at Carnegie-Mellon University. From Wright he learned the language of organic architecture, which he has practiced from Seattle for nearly forty years. The simplicity of his forms has allowed him to produce exquisite residences that respond to the site and the client's distinctive requirements yet are economical.

One of Stricker's larger commissions is the 1989 retirement home for Jean and Frank Fisher. They selected a site in a newly subdivided area that had been a ranch in Sisters, Oregon. Wagon trains once passed by on the nearby Oregon Trail. The area's history and Jean Fisher's native American ancestry led the architect to create a design symbolically reflecting this combined heritage. He proposed a tepee-shaped living area in a plan based on a hexagonal module.

The 3,200 square feet of space is enveloped in beveled cedar siding that alternates wide and narrow bands. The broad cedar-shake roof is an earthy companion to the rock-strewn terrain, marked by tall ponderosa pines and sagebrush. An old pine snag, or stump, on the site became the source of the house's color scheme; within its weathered rings were shades of tan and gold, orange, and even red. A local salishan stone was massed for the towering central fireplace and supporting piers.

An angled garage wing joins the house to create the entrance. Inside, the open plan reveals itself. No corridors waste space. The living room reaches to the top of the tepee shape, anchored by the fireplace. Built-in and free-standing furniture designed for the home continues the flow. It is a complete design, one Wright would no doubt have recognized as grown from the seeds he planted so long ago.

Opposite: Looking from the den into the open living area, the fluidity and unity of the spaces are clear. Triangular shapes produced by the house's hexagonal module create unusual interconnected and dynamic rooms. The living area soars to the top of its tepee ceiling and out like a ship's prow.

Top: Horizontal courses of beveled cedar siding emphasize the outreaching angular forms.

Bottom: A triangular master bathroom opens through french doors to the terrace and ponderosa pines beyond. [Photographs by Randy Shelton, Architectural Images]

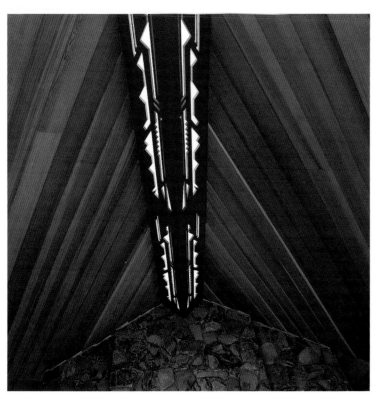

Radiating from the center of a salishan stone fireplace is a decorative ceiling light screen—an abstraction of the nearby Sisters mountain range, the town of Sisters, and the profile of the residence itself.

The massive fireplace rises to the top of the living room ceiling, clearly defining the hearth as the center of the house. Modular hassocks and benches, upholstered in golds and pumpkins, are clustered in various places on the wool Berber carpet. Cove lighting produces an indirect glow from the cedar-covered ceiling, while companion fixtures point down to light various areas directly.

WRIGHT AT HOME

THIS CATALOGUE PRESENTS AN ARRAY OF UNIQUE HOME FURNISHINGS THAT MAY BE PURCHASED TODAY: REPRODUCTIONS OF ORIGINAL WRIGHT DESIGNS, INSPIRATIONS FROM THEM, AND ITEMS THAT ARE COMPATIBLE WITH THE WRIGHT STYLE. SUPPLIERS ARE LISTED ON PAGES 216-217.

Liberty Rug
Liberty Magazine, 1926–1927
Frank Lloyd Wright
100% wool
Any size 6' x 9' or larger
Custom colors available
Schumacher

In 1926–1927 Wright designed a series of cover designs, one for every month, for *Liberty* magazine. The drawing for December, called "Gifts," was the basis for this rug design. The *Liberty* drawings were never published, but Wright used them as inspirations for other designs. Authorized by the Frank Lloyd Wright Foundation.

Prairie Chair
Leopold Stickley, 1910–1913
Solid quartersawn white oak
Leather or fabric upholstery
27" high, 39 1/2" wide, 35 1/2" deep
No. 89-416
Mission Oak Collection
L. and J. G. Stickley, Inc.

Prairie Settle (above right)
Leopold Stickley, 1910–1913
Solid quartersawn white oak
Leather or fabric upholstery
29" high, 84 1/2" wide, 37 1/2" deep
No. 89-220
Mission Oak Collection
L. and J. G. Stickley, Inc.

These reissues of Stickley designs show the Prairie influence. Functional yet gracefully curving corbels accentuate the bold horizontal lines while they support the 7" wraparound arms. The backs are solid wood panels. Drop-in seat cushions use foam, cotton, and Dacron for firm support. Also available in the same style is a love seat (No. 89-210).

Robie 3 Sofa (below)
Robie House, Chicago, Illinois, 1908
Frank Lloyd Wright
Two-seat sofa
Cherry in natural or walnut finish
Beech in mahogany, oak, or ebony finish
Variety of fabrics
29 7/8" high, 94" wide, 16 7/8" to seat, 25" to arm
Cassina

Wright's house for the Frederick C. Robie family is one of his finest Prairie designs. Its strong horizontal lines make it seem to hug the earth. Inside are free-flowing spaces. The living room and dining room are separated only by a two-sided fireplace, giving the impression of being a single open space. The furnishings were designed to enhance this feeling of openness.

This two-seat sofa with extended arm rests, a behind-the-seat shelf, and an upholstered seat reflects the dominant horizontals of the house itself (pages 46–47). Its unique design eliminates the need for accompanying end or back tables. The slightly flared leg is consistent with other details in the house. Authorized by the Frank Lloyd Wright Foundation.

Stickley Spindle Settle
Gustav Stickley, 1905
Solid quartersawn white oak
Various fabrics and leathers
49" high, 48 1/2" wide, 24 1/2" deep
No. 89-286
Mission Oak Collection
L. and J. G. Stickley, Inc.

"They are built on more slender lines, tall, graceful and showing an effect of quaint refinement," said Gustav Stickley in describing this newly patented spindle design. Its lighter lines are more like Prairie styles than some of the heavier Stickley items. Companion pieces include a rocker (No. 89-376R), an arm chair (No. 89-376), and a side chair (No. 89-384).

Leather Sofa *(below)*
Oil-finished cherry
79" or 56" long, 28" high, 30" deep
Light brown, dark brown, or black leather upholstery
Thos. Moser Cabinetmakers

Two versions of this Arts and Crafts–inspired design are available, one seating two and the other three persons. Both slatted models have full-grain leather cushions in a choice of colors. Their companion is the lounge chair above.

Lounge Chair
Oil-finished cherry
28" high, 30" wide, 30" deep
Various colors of leather upholstery
Thos. Moser Cabinetmakers

A companion to the Moser sofas, this comfortable square chair recalls the Arts and Crafts period in both its shape and its slatted wood sides.

Morris Chair
Gustav Stickley, 1905
Solid quartersawn white oak
Leather upholstery
40" high, 33" wide, 32 1/2" to 49" deep
No. 89-369
Mission Oak Collection
L. and J. G. Stickley, Inc.

This chair is a virtually identical reissue of a Gustav Stickley design except that it incorporates the durable quadralinear post construction later perfected by the Stickleys. The chair, a forerunner of a recliner, is similar to those Wright designed for his Prairie houses. A footstool (No. 89-395) also is available.

Midway 1 Chair
Midway Gardens, Chicago, Illinois,
1914
Frank Lloyd Wright
Hexagonal-back side chair with
upholstered seat and back
Cherry in natural or walnut finish
Beech in mahogany, oak, or ebony
finish
Variety of fabrics
34¼" high, 20¼" wide, 18⅞"
deep, 18" to seat height
Cassina

The comprehensive design for
Midway Gardens, a dining and
entertainment center that has been
demolished, included sculptures,
murals, furniture, dishes, and light
fixtures as well as the building
itself. Unfortunately, the complex,
which was inspired by the parks
and beer gardens of Europe, faced
financial hard times from the beginning, and the furnishing designs
were not executed. This chair was
designed to be used in the dining
room. Authorized by the Frank
Lloyd Wright Foundation.

Midway 2 Chair
Midway Gardens, Chicago, Illinois,
1914
Frank Lloyd Wright
Disc-shaped, steel-rod side chair
White, gray, red, or blue enamel
Upholstered, open back or vinyl
34½" high, 15¾" wide, 18½"
deep, 18¼" to seat height
Cassina

Designed by Wright for the
outdoor garden court of Midway
Gardens, this chair is a light,
filigreelike composition of triangles
and circles—one more element in
the project's overall coordinated
design. Authorized by the Frank
Lloyd Wright Foundation.

Midway 3 Table (below)
Midway Gardens, Chicago, Illinois,
1914
Frank Lloyd Wright
Glass-top dining table with steel
base
White, gray, red, or blue enamel
29" high, 47¼" square or round
top
Cassina

This airy table was created by
Wright's successor firm, Taliesin
Architects, Associated, to be a
companion for the Midway 2 chair
he designed. It repeats the triangular motif in the base of the chair.

Friedman Armchair and Stool
Friedman House, Bannockburn,
Illinois, 1956
Frank Lloyd Wright
Upholstered armchair and
footstool
Cherry in natural or walnut finish
Beech in mahogany, oak, or ebony
finish
Variety of fabrics
Chair: 28½" high, 28⅞" wide,
27½" deep, 15½" to seat height
Footstool: 15½" high, 23¼" wide,
23¼" deep, 15½" to seat height
Cassina

This armchair and its accompanying
footstool, designed for Allen
Friedman, are a refinement of two
earlier designs, one for Wright's
son David Wright in 1951 and a
prototype for the Kaufmann store
offices in 1935. Wright also had
three made for his office at Taliesin
(page 220). Authorized by the
Frank Lloyd Wright Foundation.

Barrel Chair
Martin House, Buffalo, New York, 1904
Frank Lloyd Wright
Arm chair with curved back and upholstered seat
Cherry in natural or walnut finish
Beech in mahogany, oak, or ebony finish
Variety of fabrics
31³/₄" high, 21¹/₂" wide, 21⁷/₈" deep
Cassina

Wright designed the first version of this chair, made of oak, for the Darwin D. Martins' house (page 79). This version was produced for Herbert Johnson's home, Wingspread, in Racine, Wisconsin, in 1937 (page 102). When Wright saw the chairs, he ordered a dozen for his own living room at Taliesin (pages 60–61). Authorized by the Frank Lloyd Wright Foundation.

Taliesin Chair
Taliesin West, Scottsdale, Arizona, 1949
Frank Lloyd Wright
Lounge chair with upholstered seat
Veneered, laminated plywood frame
Cherry in natural or walnut finish
Beech in mahogany, oak, or ebony finish
Variety of fabrics
30¹/₄" high, 37" wide, 35¹/₂" deep, 14⁷/₈" to seat height
Cassina

This chair, designed for his own living room at Taliesin West (pages 66–67), exemplifies Wright's break with traditional construction methods. Instead of uprights, crosspieces, and frames, he handled stress with a system of multilayered plywood planes. Resembling folded butterflies, the chairs continued the house's dominant triangular theme. Limited availability. Authorized by the Frank Lloyd Wright Foundation.

Coonley Chair
Coonley House, Riverside, Illinois, 1907
Frank Lloyd Wright
Upholstered side chair
Cherry in natural or walnut finish
Beech in mahogany, oak, or ebony finish
Variety of fabrics
27¹/₂" high, 16⁷/₈" wide, 18¹/₂" deep, 18¹/₈" to seat height
Cassina

Designed for the Avery Coonleys' house, one of Wright's most complex and beautifully articulated residences, this chair is similar to those Wright designed for the Dana, Husser, and Clark houses as well as for his own use. It has an upholstered seat and slatted back, but this version is shorter and has a less formal appearance. Authorized by the Frank Lloyd Wright Foundation.

Purcell Chair
Purcell-Cutts House, Minneapolis, Minnesota, 1913
William Purcell and George Elmslie
Quartersawn white oak
Leather upholstery
33¹/₈" high, 24¹/₈" wide, 22" deep
Peter Korab Studios

Two chairs designed for this house (pages 160–161) were reproduced when it was restored by the Minneapolis Institute of Arts. Duplicates have been made available to benefit further restoration efforts. Both chairs have thirty-four spindles and dozens of little blocks, but the half-back version has only a small upholstered pad on the back.

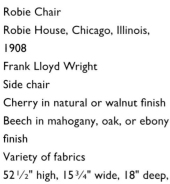

Robie Chair
Robie House, Chicago, Illinois, 1908
Frank Lloyd Wright
Side chair
Cherry in natural or walnut finish
Beech in mahogany, oak, or ebony finish
Variety of fabrics
52 1/2" high, 15 3/4" wide, 18" deep, 18 1/2" to seat height
Cassina

This high-back side chair with vertical wooden slats offered a contrast in the strongly horizontal house. When all of the chairs were grouped at the table, they created a smaller room within the surrounding room. Authorized by the Frank Lloyd Wright Foundation.

Dana-Thomas Chair
Dana-Thomas House, Springfield, Illinois, 1904
Frank Lloyd Wright
Dining room chair
Oak
Leather upholstery
51" high, 17" wide, 18" deep
Dana-Thomas House Foundation

This stately, vertical slat-back dining room chair is a reproduction of originals that Wright designed for Susan Lawrence Dana's elegant house, where she entertained frequently in the dramatic dining space (page 71). Also available is a reproduction of a small oak dining table like those Wright designed to extend the Dana house's dining area. It has a cantilevered square top with vertical slats on two sides of the base and connecting cross stretchers.

Prairie Dining Room Chair
Quartersawn white oak
Leather upholstery
46 1/2" high, 18" wide, 19 1/4" deep
David Heinz Studio

Strongly influenced by Louis Sullivan, the three-story house built in 1897 for Isidore Heller of Chicago was one of Wright's early commissions. Its scale and interior detailing inspired a new custom design for a dining room set for recent owners, who did not have access to any original Wright-designed furniture. This chair is part of the set.

Dining Chair
Quartersawn white oak and ebony
Leather upholstery
46" high, 18" wide, 20" deep
David Heinz Studio

This Arts and Crafts–style chair owes its inspiration to three designers: Wright, Charles Rennie Mackintosh, and Greene and Greene. The Scottish designer Mackintosh is noted for attenuated furniture designs, including high-back chairs like Wright designed. Preeminent architects of luxurious bungalows, the Greene brothers used incomparable craftsmanship both in their houses and in the furniture that filled them. The delicate quality of this chair makes it seem almost musical, an attribute that Wright would have liked.

Reader's Table *(above)*
Oil-finished cherry
110" or 134" long, 48" wide,
30" high
Thos. Moser Cabinetmakers

Inspired by Wright, this dramatic
table has a series of three parallel
posts that create a Prairie look.
It is well suited to a large space
and can be paired with Moser's
Reader's Side Chair, which was
designed to complement the table.
It has a medium-high slatted back
and an upholstered seat, available
in leather or your choice of fabric.

Taliesin Dining Table *(below)*
Taliesin, Spring Green, Wisconsin,
1925
Frank Lloyd Wright
Rectangular dining table
Cherry in natural or walnut finish
Beech in mahogany, oak, or ebony
finish
75 1/2" or 98" long, 38 1/2" wide,
27 1/2" high
Cassina

Wright designed this table for his
own use in the area that served as
both living room and dining room
at Taliesin in Spring Green, Wisconsin (pages 60–61). It was used
by the Wright family and their con-
tinual flow of guests from 1925 to
1959. The table is shown with the
Coonley Chairs (page 195), but
Wright surrounded this dramatic
rectangular piece with the barrel-

shaped chairs (page 195) he
created for the Martin house in
Buffalo. The contrasting shapes,
against the backdrop of the natural
limestone wall, produced a dynamic
yet cozy alcove nestled in the large
open area where the Wrights
gathered. Authorized by the Frank
Lloyd Wright Foundation.

Ford Dining Room Server *(above)*
Ford House, Pasadena, California,
1907
Greene and Greene
Mahogany and ebony
28" high, 78" wide, 21" deep
James-Randell Reproductions

Using construction and finishing
methods established by Greene
and Greene, this reproduction represents the elegant simplicity of the
architects' furniture designs.

Stickley Sideboard *(below)*
L. and J. G. Stickley, 1912
Solid quartersawn white oak
46 1/2" high, 60" wide, 22" deep
No. 89-711
Mission Oak Collection
L. and J. G. Stickley, Inc.

This Stickley reproduction is a
noteworthy example of Prairie
design and influence. The long, low
shelf, the plate rail with squares,
and the width itself all emphasize a
horizontal line, straightforward
proportions, and structural

integrity. Its construction reveals
the ray flake of the quartersawn
oak on all four surfaces. The
butterfly inlay on the doors is the
Craftsman idea of making things
"closely associated with our daily
life and surroundings."

Atlantis Table
Console or dining table
Oak, glass, and black lacquer
63" square, 29" high shown
Custom design
David Orth Architectural Furniture

This custom-designed table was completed in 1987 for the Larson house, a Prairie Style design in Maywood, Illinois, by architects Tallmadge and Watson, turn-of-the-century contemporaries of Wright; it also has been used as a foyer table in the Young house in Oak Park, Illinois, which was remodeled by Wright in 1895. The plate glass appears to hover over the neo-Prairie Style legs, supported by black arches. In a similar style, David Orth also has designed a large dining table with the same leg motif as this table, in silver gray bird's-eye maple.

New Century Round Table Forty
Oil-finished cherry
40" diameter, 29" high
Thos. Moser Cabinetmakers

This table will seat four comfortably, for games or dining, and works well as an occasional table. With its vertical slats and curved crosspieces, it uses key Arts and Crafts elements. Also available is a smaller 20" table, Round Stand Twenty.

Square Dining Table *(below)*
Quartersawn white oak and ebony
60" square, 30" high
David Heinz Studio

The influence of both Wright and the architects Greene and Greene can be seen in this sturdy oak table with special flair.

Allen Table
Allen House, Wichita, Kansas, 1917
Frank Lloyd Wright
Rectangular dining table
Cherry in natural or walnut finish
Beech in mahogany, oak, or ebony finish
101¼" or 110¼" long, 41¾" wide, 27¾" high
Cassina

The cantilevered horizontal lines of this table designed for the Henry J. Allens are typical of Wright's Prairie Style furniture. Two versions seat six or eight persons. Authorized by the Frank Lloyd Wright Foundation.

Console Table
Rosa satinwood and rosewood
45" long, 13" wide, 32" high shown
Custom design
David Orth Architectural Furniture

Horizontal and vertical elements, recalling the Prairie Style, have been merged with a restrained biomorphism to produce this delicate, taut form, which seems to rise out of the ground. Prairie designs also are called up in a three-post coffee table from David Orth, a free-form creation with a cantilevered top.

New Century Coffee Table *(above right)*
Oil-finished cherry
48" long, 30" wide, 19" high
Thos. Moser Cabinetmakers

The five vertical slats on the end panels are a contemporary interpretation of Arts and Crafts designs. This table is slightly higher than most coffee tables and is compatible with the Moser leather sofas and chair (page 193).

Robie Table and Stool *(below)*
Robie House, Chicago, Illinois, 1908
Frank Lloyd Wright
Cherry in natural or walnut finish
Beech in mahogany, oak, or ebony finish
Variety of fabrics
35 3/4" wide and deep, 16 1/8" high, or 14 1/8" wide and deep, 16 1/8" high
Cassina

The square table (with the choice of a wood or glass top) and the smaller stool version are character-

istic of the Robie house designs, which were coordinated by George Niedecken. The vertical legs pierce the horizontal plane of the lower shelf and repeat the flared leg seen in the sofa design (page 192). The large table serves as a coffee table, while the smaller one, with a wood top, may be used as a footstool or an occasional table. Both of these dramatic reproductions recall the strongly horizontal lines and detailing of the Robie house itself. Authorized by the Frank Lloyd Wright Foundation.

Stickley Drop Leaf Table
Leopold Stickley
Solid quartersawn white oak
8" wide, 24" deep, 24 1/2" high
closed; 24" wide, 24" deep open
No. 89-509
Mission Oak Collection
L. and J. G. Stickley, Inc.

This reissue is a perfect companion
for the reclining Morris chair (page
193). The classic shoe foot sup-
ports the cut-out slab sides, which
are joined by a through-tenoned
shelf. When open, the two drop
leaves form a square table.

Stickley Round Table
Gustav Stickley
Solid quartersawn white oak
29" diameter, 28 1/2" high
No. 89-663
Mission Oak Collection
L. and J. G. Stickley, Inc.

A favorite Gustav Stickley design,
this table often appeared in suggested interiors featured in his
Craftsman magazine. The round top
is supported by cross stretchers
that are tenoned into the legs.

New Century Side Table with Shelf
(below)
Oil-finished cherry
20" square, 27" high
Thos. Moser Cabinetmakers

Next to a chair or bed or in a
hallway, this is a versatile small
table with a drawer and lower
shelf. It is a good companion to
other items in the Moser line.

New Century Book Table
Oil-finished cherry
32" square, 29" high
Shelves: 10 1/4" high, 10" deep
Thos. Moser Cabinetmakers

An interpretation of a useful
Stickley design, this square table
includes 8 1/2 linear feet of book
storage on all four sides. The
vertical divider posts are a
common Prairie and Arts and
Crafts motif. A more standard
bookshelf with open shelves, 32"
high, 42 1/4 wide, and 10" deep,
also is available.

Stickley Tall Case Clock
Leopold Stickley, 1910
Solid quartersawn white oak
Solid brass-etched dial
80" high, 27" wide, 16" deep
No. 89-86
Mission Oak Collection
L. and J. G. Stickley, Inc.

A Prairie Style flat-top clock, this distinctive piece features exposed mortise-and-tenon joinery pinned with oak dowels and strikes on the hour and half hour. A reissue, it varies from the original design in that it has removable side panels to permit access to the handmade, signed movement. The clock face, a series of square motifs set into the circle, Includes a solid brass dial like the original with the legend "L. and J. G. Stickley — Handcraft — Manlius, N.Y."

New Century Study Carrel
(above left)
Oil-finshed cherry
54" high, 52" wide, 30" deep
Thos. Moser Cabinetmakers

Inspired by the study table Wright designed for the first Little house of 1903 in Peoria, Illinois, this modern version accommodates a computer and can be wired if desired. Pressed black concrete is used as the work surface to withstand heavy use. The carrel is suitable for the home, an office, or a university library. Like other Moser furniture, this item is made of cherry rather than the oak seen in many pieces of the period. The cherry develops a patina over time, colored by air and sunlight. Natural oil finishes bring out the beauty of the wood, which has different but carefully matched grain patterns in various items.

Stickley Executive Desk
Solid quartersawn white oak
Solid cast-copper hardware
30" high, 72" wide, 36" deep
No. 89-2272
Mission Oak Collection
L. and J. G. Stickley, Inc.

This executive desk is a new design influenced by the Prairie School. It features pedestal drawer locks, two file drawers, a modesty panel, and a pencil tray. Arts and Crafts furniture like the Stickley items that are made with quartersawn oak are distinguished by wavy woodgrain lines or ray flakes. Glassy rays in the oak also bind together the perpendicular fibers and give the wood its great strength.

Stickley Armoire–Television Cabinet
Solid quartersawn white oak
78" high, 48" wide, 24" deep
No. 89-1127
Mission Oak Collection
L. and J. G. Stickley, Inc.

"Never do a thing unless something justifies it . . . let your design grow out of necessity," said Gustav Stickley. This philosophy set the foundation for a newly designed armoire or entertainment center that features butterfly inlays, pinned-through tenons, and Prairie Style moldings. As an armoire, it is available with shelves and drawers; as an entertainment or television unit, it includes upper pocket doors that conceal a television slide and swivel mechanism and a videocassette recorder compartment.

Stickley Triple Dresser
Solid quartersawn white oak
Cast-copper hardware
35 1/2" high, 66" wide, 20" deep
No. 89-625
Mission Oak Collection
L. and J. G. Stickley, Inc.

Adapted from an earlier Stickley design, this dresser features exposed mortise-and-tenon joinery pinned with oak dowels. Drawers are handfitted, and the crest rail may be monogrammed and dated.

New Century China Bed (below)
Oil-finished cherry
85 1/2" long, 65" or 81" wide, 42" high
Boxspring and mattress: 21" high
Thos. Moser Cabinetmakers

In this bed, space is defined by vertical and horizontal lines, an ancient idea still relevant today, as it was during Wright's era. The headboard and footboard are removable.

Mantel Clock
Peter Hansen, 1910
Solid quartersawn white oak
8-day, solid-brass German clock movement
22" high, 16" wide, 8" deep
No. 89-85
Mission Oak Collection
L. and J. G. Stickley, Inc.

Unadorned geometric shapes—trapezoidal, circular, rectangular, and square—are unified in this design by Peter Hansen, Stickley's famous designer. The clock is characteristic of pure Arts and Crafts designs that are compatible with Wright's. The quartersawn oak grain gives the clock a special patina.

Bogk House Rug
Bogk House, Milwaukee,
Wisconsin, 1916
Frank Lloyd Wright
100% wool
Any size 6' x 9' or larger
Custom colors available
Schumacher

Featuring a geometric, cross-
shaped motif, this design is an
adaptation of a carpet in Wright's
Bogk house (pages 132–133). The
small decorative squares echo the
detailing of the furniture, which
also was designed for the home.
Authorized by the Frank Lloyd
Wright Foundation.

Imperial Arrow Rug
Imperial Hotel, Tokyo, Japan,
1915–1922
Frank Lloyd Wright
100% wool
Any size 6' x 9' or larger
Custom colors available
Schumacher

Wright's design for the Imperial
Hotel was one of the most ambi-
tious of his career. The richly ornamented building was constructed of
native oya, a lava stone. It became
famous when it survived the earthquake of 1923 with little damage.
Tragically, it was demolished in
1967 to make room for a larger
hotel. This rug is an adaptation of a
large, square rug designed by
Wright for one of the hotel guest
rooms. In the original design, the
arrow motif was repeated in all
four corners. Authorized by the
Frank Lloyd Wright Foundation.

Imperial Triangle Rug
Imperial Hotel, Tokyo, Japan,
1915–1922
Frank Lloyd Wright
100% wool
Any size 6' x 9' or larger
Custom colors available
Schumacher

Originally a corner motif in a large,
square rug at the Imperial Hotel,
the design has been modified to
create an all-over triangular
pattern. Authorized by the Frank
Lloyd Wright Foundation.

May House Rug
May House, Grand Rapids,
Michigan, 1908
Frank Lloyd Wright
Handtufted wool
Various sizes
Custom design
PWV Studios, Ltd.

This carpet is an example of several
reproductions made exclusively for
the restoration of Wright's May
house (pages 82–83). The square
and abstracted leaf motifs here are
repeated throughout the house.
The carpet is only a sample of the
work of the artisans and is not
available for sale.

Coonley Rug No. 1
Coonley House, Riverside, Illinois, 1908
Frank Lloyd Wright
100% wool
Any size 6' x 9' or larger
Custom colors available
Schumacher

The Avery Coonleys selected Wright as their architect because they believed that his houses reflected "the countenence of principle." The house he designed for them had an elaborate decorative scheme, including the designs on which this and another Schumacher rug (Coonley No. 2) are based. Authorized by the Frank Lloyd Wright Foundation.

Building Blocks Rug
100% wool
Various sizes and colors
Custom design
Weskuske

With its interplay of geometric shapes, primarily squares, this design shows its inspirations in motifs favored by Wright and Mondrian. It is one example of the work of this studio.

Herald Square Rug
Handtufted wool
Various colors, shapes, and sizes
Custom design
Edward Fields, Inc.

The geometry and color combination shown here are reminiscent of Wright's art glass window designs. Using simple shapes and linear elements, this rug is one of the Wright-inspired compositions that are available in the portfolio of the manufacturer.

Heurtley Rug
Heurtley House, Oak Park, Illinois, 1902
Frank Lloyd Wright
100% wool
Any size 6' x 9' or larger
Custom colors available
Schumacher

The Heurtley house remained a favorite of Wright—"one of my best," he wrote the owner fifty years later. This striking rug is adapted from a design for a runner there. Authorized by the Frank Lloyd Wright Foundation.

Imperial Triangles II *(top)*
Imperial Hotel, Tokyo, Japan,
1915–1922
Frank Lloyd Wright
60% cotton, 40% rayon
54" wide
7 colorways
Schumacher

Featuring triangles, a favorite
among the many geometric motifs
that Wright liked to use, this
woven fabric design was created
for the architect's famous hotel in
Tokyo, which was torn down in
1967. Authorized by the Frank
Lloyd Wright Foundation.

Imperial Squares *(bottom)*
Imperial Hotel, Tokyo, Japan,
1915–1922
Frank Lloyd Wright
38% wool, 36% cotton, 18% acrylic,
8% rayon
55" wide
6 colorways
Schumacher

Another reproduction from the
architecturally rich Imperial Hotel,
this textile is part of the interrelated decorative designs Wright
executed for the sprawling hotel.
Authorized by the Frank Lloyd
Wright Foundation.

Liberty Weave *(left)*
Liberty Magazine, 1926–1927
Frank Lloyd Wright
100% spun rayon
51" wide
4 colorways
Schumacher

From the twelve covers that
Wright designed for *Liberty* magazine in 1926–1927, all of them
graphic designs representing the
changing seasons, a segment of one
cover was used as the inspiration
for this intricate weave. Authorized by the Frank Lloyd Wright
Foundation.

March Balloons *(right)*
Liberty Magazine, 1926–1927
Frank Lloyd Wright
78% rayon, 12% cotton, 10%
polyester
55" wide
5 colorways
Schumacher

Liberty magazine again was the
source for this playful motif. Taken
from an unpublished cover design,
the fabric is a luxurious jacquard.
The scale has been slightly reduced
from the original cover graphic.
Authorized by the Frank Lloyd
Wright Foundation.

Imperial Squares, shown at the
bottom, is described at left.

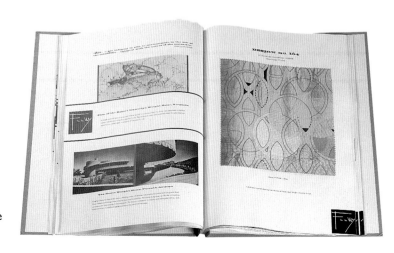

In 1955 Wright designed a collection of fabrics and wall coverings
for Schumacher that was called the
Taliesin Line.

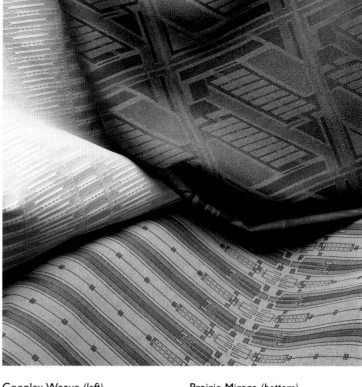

Prairie Fern *(left)*
Coonley House, Riverside, Illinois,
1908
Frank Lloyd Wright
100% wool damask
54" wide
7 colorways
Schumacher

This subtle, geometric design is based on the carved grille that covers the indirect lighting in this important house designed by Wright. Authorized by the Frank Lloyd Wright Foundation.

Imperial Crystals *(right)*
Imperial Hotel, Tokyo, Japan,
1915–1922
Frank Lloyd Wright
50% wool, 50% cotton
54" wide
6 colorways
Schumacher

Taken also from Wright's dramatic Imperial Hotel in Tokyo, this pattern is similar to Imperial Triangles II but has a different fabric content. Authorized by the Frank Lloyd Wright Foundation.

Tulip Tapestry *(bottom)*
Coonley House, Riverside, Illinois,
1908
Frank Lloyd Wright
70% cotton, 27% wool, 3% nylon
54" wide
7 colorways
Schumacher

Derived from another design by Wright for the Avery Coonleys, this tulip motif fabric was adapted from unexecuted studies for tile inlay work on the house's exterior. Authorized by the Frank Lloyd Wright Foundation.

Coonley Weave *(left)*
Coonley House, Riverside, Illinois,
1908
Frank Lloyd Wright
100% Cotton
54" wide
6 colorways
Schumacher

Wright worked closely with the Avery Coonleys to design numerous decorative arts for their house. This tightly woven fabric is taken from the house's carpet pattern. Authorized by the Frank Lloyd Wright Foundation.

Prairie Mirage *(bottom)*
Coonley House, Riverside, Illinois,
1908
Frank Lloyd Wright
100% cotton
54" wide
3 colorways
Schumacher

The Coonley house carpet also was the inspiration for the dramatic Prairie Mirage motif. Authorized by the Frank Lloyd Wright Foundation.

Prairie Fern, shown at right, is described at left.

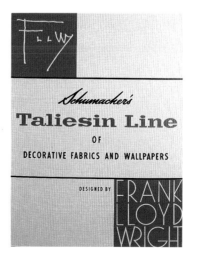

The cover of the 1955 Taliesin Line catalogue for Schumacher features Wright's favorite red and his signature block.

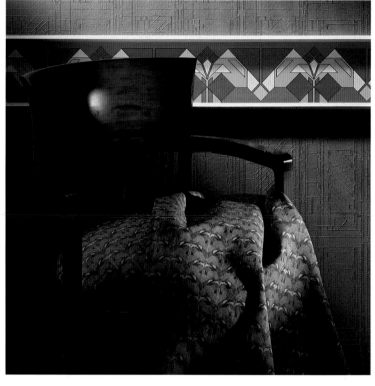

Hoffman Ring Border
Liberty Magazine, 1926–1927
Frank Lloyd Wright
Handprinted on paper
5" high
5 colorways
Schumacher

This border was derived from an original drawing by Wright for the cover of *Liberty* magazine. While the drawing was never published, it became the source of many designs, including the rug for the Hoffman house in Rye, New York, designed by Wright in 1954. The border coordinates with other Schumacher wallpaper designs. A related design, March Balloons, is available as a fabric (page 206). Authorized by the Frank Lloyd Wright Foundation.

This detail from Wright's March *Liberty* magazine cover shows his fondness for geometric—even playful—shapes and bright colors.

Triangular Tulip Border *(top)*
Coonley House, Riverside, Illinois, 1908
Frank Lloyd Wright
Handprinted on paper
7" high
4 colorways
Schumacher

Like a number of the Schumacher fabrics, this stylized geometric wallpaper border comes from the decoratively rich residence Wright created for the Avery Coonleys. It is based on exterior tilework at the house. Authorized by the Frank Lloyd Wright Foundation.

Allen Ceiling Grille *(bottom)*
Allen House, Wichita, Kansas, 1917
Frank Lloyd Wright
Embossed fabric-backed vinyl
27" or 54" wide
9 colorways
Schumacher

For the house he designed for the Henry J. Allens, Wright drew a carved wooden grille for the dining room ceiling. It was designed to filter light onto the table through the grille pattern, creating the same kind of subtle visual interest that this side wall creates. Authorized by the Frank Lloyd Wright Foundation.

Taliesin Frieze Border *(top)*
Taliesin, Spring Green, Wisconsin,
1911–1959
Frank Lloyd Wright
Handprinted on paper
5 1/2" high
4 colorways
Schumacher

The Taliesin frieze was inspired by
elements of Wright's own Wisconsin home, where geometric patterns in the furnishings, art glass,
decorative arts, and carpets are a
counterpoint to vistas of his favorite Spring Green countryside.
Authorized by the Frank Lloyd
Wright Foundation.

Autobiography *(bottom)*
An Autobiography, 1943
Frank Lloyd Wright
Embossed fabric-backed vinyl
27" or 54" wide
10 colorways
Schumacher

The endpaper of Wright's autobiography, which he designed himself,
provided the idea for this pattern.
His first autobiography, published
in 1932, was written during barren
years in his career but eventually
encouraged new interest in
Wright's work. Authorized by the
Frank Lloyd Wright Foundation.

Hoffman Key Border *(top)*
Hoffman House, Rye, New York,
1954
Frank Lloyd Wright
5" high
Handprinted on paper
8 colorways
Schumacher

This border pattern was inspired by
one of the linear motifs on a runner
that accompanied the large rug in
the Hoffman house. Authorized by
the Frank Lloyd Wright Foundation.

Cloud Block *(bottom)*
Hoffman House, Rye, New York,
1954
Frank Lloyd Wright
Embossed fabric-backed vinyl
27" or 54" wide
10 colorways
Schumacher

Cloud Block takes elements of the
Hoffman house rug as its design
inspiration. Authorized by the
Frank Lloyd Wright Foundation.

Huntington Ceiling Mount
Hanging ceiling light
Solid brass, vertigris copper finish
Iridescent glass in 4 colors
7" high, 27 1/2" wide, 17 1/2" deep,
30" overall
No. HCM-27GW
Arroyo Craftsman

This ceiling light is one of a series
of fixtures inspired by Greene and
Greene and Frank Lloyd Wright.
Their clean lines and design simplicity make them suitable in a
variety of settings. Chain-mounted
and flush-mounted versions also
are available.

Huntington Sconce *(below)*
Wall-mounted light
Solid brass, antique brass finish
4 types of glass
12" high, 6 1/2" wide, 4 1/2" deep
No. MS 12WO-AB
Arroyo Craftsman

Several similar styles and sizes
of wall-mounted fixtures in the
Prairie Style are available, all
suitable for interior or exterior
use. This version directs light both
up and down. A roofed model
throws light only down.

Mission Garden Light
Post light
Solid brass, vertigris copper finish
12 1/2" high, 7" square
No. MP-7GW
Arroyo Craftsman

Suited for garden paths, gateways,
and entries, this post-mounted
fixture comes in three sizes.
Similar fixtures are available in
hanging wall-mounted and flush-
mounted versions.

Stamford Light
Exterior wall light
Solid brass, vertigris copper finish
Several sizes from 7" to 11" wide
No. 764A
Brass Light Gallery

The original design for this outside
fixture was used in Prairie and
Craftsman residences from about
1905 to 1925. It is available with
various art glass panel colors.

Desk Lamp
Solid brass, vertigris copper finish
18" high
No. 767F
Brass Light Gallery

This Craftsman lantern from the Arts and Crafts period is available with a choice of colors for the art glass panels.

Craftsman Pendant
Light on chain
Solid brass
12" high, 5" wide
No. 765A
Brass Light Gallery

Suspended from an articulated rectangular chain with various colored art glass panels, the Craftsman Pendant was originally used in Prairie and Arts and Crafts homes of the 1905–1920 period.

Culbertson Light (below)
Wall lantern
Culbertson House, 1907
Greene and Greene
Mahogany with ebony details
Tiffany-style iridescent glass
14 1/2" high, 10" wide, 7" deep
James-Randell Reproductions

An interior wall lantern, this design is reminiscent of Prairie Style fixtures of the period. It is one of many the architects designed for their residential commissions.

Dearborn Light
Ceiling fixture
Solid brass, various finishes
16" wide, variable height
No. 762C
Brass Light Gallery

This design is a more highly stylized dining room ceiling fixture, with an articulated rectangular chain and Craftsman-style lanterns. The art glass panels are iridescent gold and white.

Sherman Park Sconce
Double-light sconce
Solid brass, vertigris copper finish
9" high, 12" wide, 7" deep
No. 754A
Brass Light Gallery

This wall sconce was a standard design used in many Prairie Style and Arts and Crafts buildings in the first two decades of the century. The glass is sandblasted, with a frosted finish. It can be mounted up or down. The fixture's design is similar to the Double-Arm Lamp described at right and to other designs not shown, including the Evanston, a single-light sconce; the Sherman Park, a double-arm ceiling light; and the Oak Park, a four-arm chandelier.

Double-Arm Lamp
Table lamp
Solid brass, various finishes
18" high, 16" wide
No. 767A
Brass Light Gallery

A simplified Prairie Style design, this desk lamp has sandblasted frosted shades. It is part of a family of period lighting fixtures offered by the company. The brass finish is shown.

Spring Green Light *(below)*
Double-light ceiling fixture
Solid brass, various finishes
8" high, 13" wide
No. 760A
Brass Light Gallery

A flush-mounted fixture suitable for a low ceiling, this light is based on an original design from 1910–1925. It also has sandblasted frosted glass.

Dana-Thomas Double Pedestal Lamp
Table lamp
Dana-Thomas House, Springfield, Illinois, 1904
Bronze base, colored glass and zinc-channel shade
23 1/4" high, 32" wide, 19" deep
Dana-Thomas House Foundation

This reproduction of a finely crafted art glass lamp designed by Wright for the Dana-Thomas house carefully replicates the detail found in the original. Also available is a similar single pedestal lamp with a sixteen-sided shade.

Tree of Life Glass *(left, bottom right)*
Martin House, Buffalo, New York,
1904
Frank Lloyd Wright
Clear, opal, and iridescent glass
40" high, 12 ¹/₂" wide or 16 ¹/₄"
high, 7 ³/₄" wide
Hooks for hanging
Frank Lloyd Wright Home and
Studio Foundation

This art glass panel was inspired by
the seven-branched "tree of life"
motif used by Wright in several
residences, most notably the house
for the Darwin Martins.

Dana-Thomas House Glass *(top right)*
Dana-Thomas House, Springfield,
Illinois, 1904
Clear and iridescent glass
16 ¹/₂" high, 5 ⁵/₈" wide
Frank Lloyd Wright Home and
Studio Foundation

Adapted from the gallery windows
of the Dana-Thomas house, this art
glass reproduction features green
iridescent glass. Other available
patterns include Playroom Glass
from Wright's Oak Park home
(page 36) and Prairie Flower Glass.

Robie House Window No. 1
Robie House, Chicago, Illinois,
1908
Frank Lloyd Wright
Clear and colored iridescent glass,
copper-channel contruction
43 ⁷/₈" high, 31 ¹/₈" wide
Oakbrook-Esser Studios

This window is one of four Robie
house patterns that have been
reproduced. The trianglular design
is an abstraction of a natural form
from the prairie and reiterates the
golden tones of the home. Authorized by the Frank Lloyd Wright
Foundation.

Lake Geneva Tulip Window *(top)*
Lake Geneva Inn, Lake Geneva,
Wisconsin, 1911
Frank Lloyd Wright
Clear and iridescent glass, zinc-
channel construction
18 ³/₄" high, 20 ⁷/₈" wide
Oakbrook-Esser Studios

The Lake Geneva Inn was a small
resort hotel designed by Wright.
The pattern in the window is
thought to be an abstraction of a
tulip. Authorized by the Frank
Lloyd Wright Foundation.

Midway Gardens Dancing Glass
Window *(bottom)*
Midway Gardens, Chicago, Illinois,
1914
Frank Lloyd Wright
Clear and flashed opal glass, zinc-
channel construction
32 ¹/₂" high, 33 ¹/₂" wide
Oakbrook-Esser Studios

For Midway Gardens, Wright
designed a series of windows
that were never constructed.
He called them "dancing glass."
Authorized by the Frank Lloyd
Wright Foundation.

Coonley Playhouse Clerestory
No. 2
Coonley Playhouse, Riverside,
Illinois, 1912
Frank Lloyd Wright
Clear and opal glass, zinc-channel
construction
33 ³/₄" high, 17 ⁷/₈" wide
Oakbrook-Esser Studios

One of five reproductions of
windows Wright designed for the
school (pages 128–129), the
patterns are thought to have been
inspired by the confetti, balloons,
and flags of a parade. The windows
can be used architecturally, dis-
played on a wall, or suspended
from the ceiling. Authorized by the
Frank Lloyd Wright Foundation.

Stork Panel
Frank Lloyd Wright Home and
Studio, Oak Park, Illinois, 1889
Frank Lloyd Wright
Plaster with bronze-painted finish
35" high, 14 1/2" wide, 3 1/2" deep
Frank Lloyd Wright Home and
Studio Foundation

Wright designed these column
capitals at the entrance (page 35)
to his Oak Park studio in 1898
to symbolize the architect's profession. The reproductions,
like the originals, are finished to
resemble bronze.

Oak Park Panel (top)
Frank Lloyd Wright Home and
Studio, Oak Park, Illinois, 1889
Frank Lloyd Wright
Plaster
29" square
Frank Lloyd Wright Home and
Studio Foundation

This decorative panel used by
Wright in his Oak Park living room
ceiling, dating from 1889, is similar
to others in the Auditorium
Theater, on which Wright was
working for Adler and Sullivan at
the time.

Freeman House Block (bottom)
Freeman House, Los Angeles,
California, 1925
Frank Lloyd Wright
Concrete
16" high, 16" wide, 3 1/2" deep
Freeman House

Two versions of the concrete block
that was used for the house have
been reproduced; one is perforated to allow light through. The
pattern depicts the house on its
triangular site within a grove of
eucalyptus trees.

Skyscraper Vase
1907
Frank Lloyd Wright
Natural terra cotta or white glaze
23" high, 6 3/4" wide, 3 1/2" deep
Tiffany and Company

This vase, apparently not developed for a specific project, was
first seen in a 1907 exhibit of
Wright's work in Chicago. It may
have originated as a design for a
building and was reworked into
this highly architectonic creation.
Authorized by the Frank Lloyd
Wright Foundation.

Oak Park Candlesticks
Frank Lloyd Wright Home and
Studio, Oak Park, Illinois, 1889
Frank Lloyd Wright
Solid oak
22 3/4" high
Frank Lloyd Wright Home and
Studio Foundation

Full-scale reproductions of the
balusters from the barrel-vaulted
1895 playroom of Wright's Oak
Park home (pages 6–7) have been
adapted as candlesticks. Their geometric composition exemplifies the
simplicity and purity of Wright's
design for the spectacular space.

Crystal Candlesticks
Leerdam Glassfabrik Company,
1920s
Frank Lloyd Wright
Lead crystal
3 1/2" or 6" high
Tiffany and Company

In the late 1920s Wright was asked by a Dutch glassmaker to create a line of tabletop items for commercial production. Only one, a flower vase, was ever produced. Now thirteen of the designs have been reproduced. These tall and short candlesticks are representative of the polygonal silver and crystal designs available from Tiffany, all of which have strongly architectonic patterns. Authorized by the Frank Lloyd Wright Foundation.

Imperial Hotel Dinner Service *(above)*
Imperial Hotel, Tokyo, Japan, 1922
Frank Lloyd Wright
Fine porcelain with gold
6 pieces per setting
Tiffany and Company

This set, designed for the formal main dining room of the Imperial Hotel, has a subdued, elegant pattern. It was first used in 1922 and was reproduced only recently, making it available for the first time outside the hotel.

Imperial Hotel Cabaret Dinner Service *(below)*
Imperial Hotel, Tokyo, Japan,
1922–1933
Frank Lloyd Wright
Fine porcelain
7 pieces per setting
Tiffany and Company

This china was created for the more informal cabaret room of the hotel. While the pattern was modified over the years, this one is the original Wright design developed in 1922 and used until 1933.

Imperial Hotel Coffee Service
Salt and Pepper Shakers
Imperial Hotel, Tokyo, Japan, 1922
Frank Lloyd Wright
Sterling silver
Tiffany and Company

These elegant table service items were used in the main dining room of the Imperial Hotel beginning in 1922. The clean geometry of the octagonal shapes repeats the forms used in the hotel. The salt and pepper shakers actually were developed as part of Wright's work for the Leerdam Glassfabrik Company, but they use a motif compatible with the hotel's coffee service. The three-piece coffee set includes a pot (with wood handle), a creamer, and a sugar bowl.

DECORATIVE ARTS SUPPLIERS

Listed below are suppliers of the furnishings presented in the catalogue as well as other compatible items.

Arroyo Craftsman
4509 Little John Street
Baldwin Park, California 91706
818-960-9411

Arroyo Craftsman creates original lighting fixtures inspired by the Arts and Crafts and Prairie School movements. Combining unique designs, quality materials, and skillful construction, the fixtures bridge inside and outside environments as easily as past and present.

Brass Light Gallery
131 South First Street
Milwaukee, Wisconsin 53204
414-271-8300

This manufacturer of quality lighting specializes in reproductions of historic styles, particularly of the early twentieth century. It also sells and restores antique lighting fixtures.

Cassina S.p.A.
155 East 56th Street
New York, New York 10022
800-770-3568
or
Wright Decorative Designs
Customer Service
800-343-9066

Cassina, which began its masters program thirty years ago to offer faithful reproductions of classic, architect-designed furniture, is licensed by the Frank Lloyd Wright Foundation to make reproductions of Wright's furniture.

Dana-Thomas House Foundation
Sumac Shop
301 East Lawrence Avenue
Springfield, Illinois 62703
or
P.O. Box 7123
Springfield, Illinois 62791
217-744-3598

The Sumac Shop is located in the carriage house visitors center of the recently restored Dana-Thomas house. The shop specializes in books, gifts, and paper products relating to Frank Lloyd Wright and the Arts and Crafts era.

Edward Fields, Inc.
232 East 59th Street
New York, New York 10022
212-310-0400

Since 1935 Edward Fields has been providing handmade wool rugs and carpets for designers and architects. The company's founder worked directly with Wright on many projects, and more recently the firm has collaborated with Taliesin Architects, Associated.

Frank Lloyd Wright Home and Studio Foundation
Gingko Tree Bookshop
951 Chicago Avenue
Oak Park, Ilinois 60302
708-848-9518

The bookshop at the Frank Lloyd Wright home and studio carries an extensive collection of books, gift items, adaptations, and reproductions of Wright designs. A catalogue is available.

Freeman House
1962 Glencoe Way
Los Angeles, California 90068-3113
213-851-0671

The concrete textile block house designed for the Freemans was constructed of more than 11,000 individual blocks. To aid in restoration of the house, its owner, the University of Southern California School of Architecture, is reproducing the blocks.

David Heinz Studio
820 North Boulevard
Oak Park, Illinois 60301
708-386 5580

This versatile custom furniture shop specializes in the creation of Arts and Crafts–style furniture and cabinetry. Heinz is a self-taught artisan who is recognized for his quality workmanship and attention to detail.

James-Randell Reproductions
768 North Fair Oaks Avenue
Pasadena, California 91103-3044
818-792-5025

The craftsmanship of James Ipekjian and the knowledge of architectural historian Randell Makinson have been combined to create fine reproductions of selected works of the architects Greene and Greene. They produce, on order, other designs by the Greenes as well as custom design work.

Peter Korab Studios
641 Belleforte
Oak Park, Ilinois 60302
708-383-3038

Korab Studios makes reproductions of historic furniture, millwork, and casework as well as designer furniture. Clients include the Frank Lloyd Wright Home and Studio Foundation, Minneapolis Institute of Arts, Chicago Art Institute, and various private residences including the Elizabeth Gale house in Oak Park, Illinois.

Mimi London, Inc.
Pacific Design Center
8687 Melrose Avenue, Suite G168
Los Angeles, California 90069
213-876-9525

This contemporary furniture company was founded by a designer who lives in a Lloyd Wright home and created log and lodgepole furniture. Among the firm's unique home furnishings are a Prairie table and several beds compatible with the Wright era.

Thos. Moser Cabinetmakers
415 Cumberland Avenue
Portland, Maine 04101
207-774-3791

Thos. Moser designs and builds finely crafted hardwood furniture suitable for contemporary or more traditional homes. Pieces are classic interpretations of early American furniture, built to order, then signed and dated by the artisan. A catalogue is available by calling or visiting showrooms in Portland, Maine (207-774-3791), Philadelphia, Pennsylvania (215-922-6440), and Alexandria, Virginia (703-548-3447).

Oakbrook-Esser Studios
129 East Wisconsin Avenue
Oconomowoc, Wisconsin 53066
800-223-5193
or
Wright Decorative Designs
Customer Service
800-343-9066

Since its founding at the turn of the century, the firm has been a leader in the design, execution, and restoration of art glass including Wright's work. It now has been licensed by the Frank Lloyd Wright Foundation to produce authentic reproductions. Some of the glass used is custom made in Europe or the company's shop using historic techniques.

David Orth Architectural Furniture
1107 Chicago Avenue
Oak Park, Illinois 60302
708-383-4399

David Orth's studio and gallery have been located in Oak Park since 1981. His fresh, nontraditional approach to furniture design has borrowed certain forms and spatial insights from Wright and employed them in the expression of his own unique vision.

PWV Studios, Ltd.
1735 Elizabeth Avenue, N.W.
Grand Rapids, Michigan 49504
616-361-5659

The studio, owned and operated by Paul and Carol V'Soske, designs and fabricates handmade wool rugs and carpeting for the architecture and design trade. The company is known for its ingenuity, skill, and attention to detail.

Schumacher
79 Madison Avenue
New York, New York 10016
800-423-5881
or
Wright Decorative Designs
Customer Service
800-343-9066
or
Paper Moon Ltd.
Brent Trading Center
390 North Circular Road, Unit 2
London NW10 OJF, England
081-451-3655

Wright began to order Schumacher fabric as early as 1909. In 1955 he designed a collection of textiles and wallpapers for the company, called the Taliesin Line. Schumacher now has been licensed by the Frank Lloyd Wright Foundation to manufacture fabrics, wall coverings, and rugs drawn from Wright's decorative designs.

L. and J. G. Stickley, Inc.
Stickley Drive
P.O. Box 480
Manlius, New York 13104-0480
315-682-5500

The Stickley family was the most well known of the Arts and Crafts furniture creators. The original company has recently reissued a line of historic Mission Oak furniture offered by Gustav and Leopold Stickley at the turn of the century. A catalogue is available.

Tiffany and Company
Fifth Avenue and 57th Street
New York, New York 10022
800-526-0649
or
Wright Decorative Designs
Customer Service
800-343-9066
or
Tiffany and Company
25 Old Bond Street
London W1X 3AA, England
071-409-2790

Tiffany has a long-standing involvement in reproductions of historically important designs. Because of its design director's special interest in the work of Wright, the company has developed a line of silver, crystal, and china items under a licensing agreement with the Frank Lloyd Wright Foundation. Many of the designs were never made in Wright's lifetime.

Weskuske
International Market Square
275 Market Street
Minneapolis, Minnesota 55405
612-339-6030

This wholesale decorator supply house specializes in fine custom rugs and carpets. Designers and architects may work with the showroom's in-house artist to develop custom designs.

ARCHITECTS AND DESIGNERS

The following design firms are represented in this book and continue to have active practices. Their projects are noted.

William Dring
Bauhs and Dring
One East Delaware Place
Suite 500
Chicago, Illinois 60611
312-649-9484

Frank Lloyd Wright home and studio (restoration chairman)

Arthur Dyson Architect
754 P Street
Suite C
Fresno, California 93721
209-486-3582

Geringer house

Hasbrouck Peterson Zimoch Sirirattumrong
104 South Michigan Avenue
Suite 250
Chicago, Illinois 60603
312-553-9600

Dana-Thomas house restoration

F. Fay Jones and Maurice Jennings Architects
619 West Dickson Street
Fayetteville, Arkansas 72701
501-443-4742

Edmondson house

Donald Kalec, Architect
5837 West Race Street
Chicago, Illinois 60644
773-287-2773

Frank Lloyd Wright home and studio (restoration director), Henderson house restoration

MacDonald and Mack Architects
712 Grain Exchange Building
Minneapolis, Minnesota 55415
612-341-4051

Purcell-Cutts house restoration

Milton Stricker Architect
3211 South Massachusetts Street
Seattle, Washington 98144
206-329-5277

Fisher house

Taliesin Architects, Associated
Scottsdale, Arizona 85261-4430
602-860-2700

Benton house

John Garrett Thorpe, AIA
1033 South Boulevard
Oak Park, Illinois 60302
708-386-1700

Frank Lloyd Wright home and studio (restoration chairman)

Tilton and Lewis
333 West Wacker Drive
Suite 200
Chicago, Illinois 60606
312-782-8333

Barr, Ingalls, May, and Zimmerman house restorations

Office of John Vinci, Inc.
1147 West Ohio Street
Chicago, Illinois 60622
312-733-7744

Coonley playhouse restoration, Frank Lloyd Wright studio (restoration architect)

Eric Lloyd Wright
24680 Piuma Road
Malibu, California 90265
818-591-8992

Auldbrass and Storer house restorations

WRIGHT HOUSES OPEN TO VISITORS

The following houses profiled or pictured in the book offer guided tours to the public. Because schedules and admission fees vary by season, please call or write for specific information. Some houses are open only by appointment.

Henry J. Allen House
255 North Roosevelt
Wichita, Kansas 67208
316-687-1027

Dana-Thomas House
301 East Lawrence Avenue
Springfield, Illinois 62703
217-782-6776

Ennis-Brown House
2655 Glendower Avenue
Los Angeles, California 90027
213-660-0607

Fallingwater
P.O. Box R
Mill Run, Pennsylvania 15464
412-329-8501

Frank Lloyd Wright
Home and Studio
951 Chicago Avenue
Oak Park, Illinois 60302
708-848-1500

Freeman House
1962 Glencoe Way
Los Angeles, California 90068-3113
213-851-0671

Hollyhock House
4808 Hollywood Boulevard
Los Angeles, California 90027
213-662-7272

Little House II (Library)
Allentown Art Museum
Fifth and Court Streets
Allentown, Pennsylvania 18105
215-432-4333

Little House II (Living Room)
Metropolitan Museum of Art
Fifth Avenue at 82nd Street
New York, New York 10028
212-879-5500, ext. 3791

May House
450 Madison, S.E.
Grand Rapids, Michigan 49503
616-246-4821

Pope-Leighey House
Woodlawn Plantation
P.O. Box 37
Mount Vernon, Virginia 22121
703-780-4000

Robie House
5757 South Woodlawn
Chicago, Illinois 60637
773-834-1362

Rosenbaum House
601 Riverview Drive
Florence, Alabama 35630
205-764-5274

Taliesin
Highway 23
Spring Green, Wisconsin 53588
608-588-2511

Taliesin West
Cactus Road and 108th Street
Scottsdale, Arizona 85261
602-860-2700

Walter House
Cedar Rock
P.O. Box One
Quasqueton, Iowa 52326
319-934-3572

Zimmerman House
c/o Currier Gallery of Art
192 Orange Street
Manchester, New Hampshire 03104
603-626-4158

FRANK LLOYD WRIGHT ORGANIZATIONS

For further information about Frank Lloyd Wright and his buildings, contact the following organizations as well as individual sites listed above.

Frank Lloyd Wright Foundation
Taliesin West
Scottsdale, Arizona 85261
602-860-2700

Frank Lloyd Wright
Building Conservancy
343 South Dearborn Street
Suite 1701
Chicago, Illinois 60604
312-663-1786

Frank Lloyd Wright
Home and Studio Foundation
951 Chicago Avenue
Oak Park, Illinois 60302
708-848-1976

FURTHER READING

Abernathy, Ann, and John Thorpe. *The Oak Park Home and Studio of Frank Lloyd Wright.* Oak Park, Illinois: Frank Lloyd Wright Home and Studio Foundation, 1988.

Brooks, H. Allen. *The Prairie School.* Toronto: University of Toronto Press, 1972.

Futagawa, Yukio, and Bruce Brooks Pfeiffer. *Frank Lloyd Wright Monographs, Studies, and Renderings.* Volumes 1–12. Tokyo: ADA Edita, Tokyo Company, Ltd., 1988.

_____. *Frank Lloyd Wright Selected Houses.* Volumes 1–8. Tokyo: ADA Edita, Tokyo Company, Ltd., 1990—.

Hanks, David A. *The Decorative Designs of Frank Lloyd Wright.* New York: E. P. Dutton, 1979.

Hanna, Paul and Jean. *Frank Lloyd Wright's Hanna House: The Clients' Report.* Carbondale, Illinois: Southern Illinois University Press, 1981.

Hitchcock, Henry-Russell. *In the Nature of Materials: The Buildings of Frank Lloyd Wright, 1887–1941.* 1942. Reprint. New York: Da Capo Press, 1973.

Jacobs, Herbert, with Catherine Jacobs. *Building with Frank Lloyd Wright: An Illustrated Memoir.* San Francisco: Chronicle Books, 1978.

Kaufmann, Edgar, Jr. *Fallingwater: A Frank Lloyd Wright Country House.* New York: Abbeville Press, 1986.

Manson, Grant Carpenter. *Frank Lloyd Wright to 1910: The First Golden Age.* New York: Van Nostrand Reinhold, 1958.

Morton, Terry B., ed. *The Pope-Leighey House.* Washington, D.C.: Preservation Press, 1969.

Sanderson, Arlene, ed. *Wright Sites: A Guide to Frank Lloyd Wright Public Places.* River Forest, Illinois: Frank Lloyd Wright Building Conservancy, 1991.

Sergeant, John. *Frank Lloyd Wright Usonian Houses.* New York: Watson-Guptil, 1975.

Tafel, Edgar. *Apprentice to Genius: Years with Frank Lloyd Wright.* New York: McGraw-Hill, 1979.

Twombly, Robert C. *Frank Lloyd Wright: An Interpretive Biography.* New York: Harper and Row, 1973.

Wright, Frank Lloyd. *An Autobiography.* New York: Duell, Sloan and Pearce, 1943. Horizon Press, 1977.

_____. *In the Cause of Architecture.* New York: McGraw-Hill, 1975.

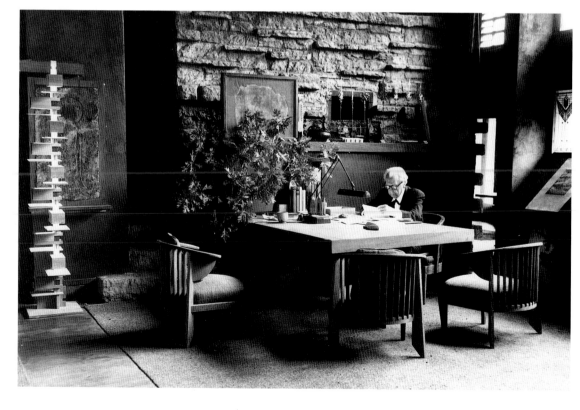

Wright reads in his office at Taliesin, surrounded by duplicates of the Friedman house chairs.
[© Frank Lloyd Wright Foundation]

INDEX

Page numbers in italics refer to illustrations.

ACKNOWLEDGMENTS

It is obvious that a book of this nature could not have been completed without the generous hospitality of the homeowners. While skilled architects have created these magical spaces—and to them I am certainly indebted—it is the owners who care for the houses and make them shine. Most of the houses included are, after all, private homes, where people eat breakfast in their pajamas and argue with their spouses. I sincerely appreciate this opportunity to step into their private lives through this "biblio-visit." Most of us must limit our quest to experience Wright interiors to visits to the numerous public buildings scattered throughout the country. They continue to survive because of the generosity and efforts of corporations, government agencies, preservation organizations, foundations, and individuals like yourself. Therefore, to all of the owners and supporters of Wright preservation projects, thank you.

The near century of scholarship on the contributions of Frank Lloyd Wright was another vital component of this inside look at Wright's houses. Special thanks are extended particularly to H. Allen Brooks, Jeffrey Chusid, Donald Hallmark, David Hanks, Donald Hoffmann, Donald Johnson, Grant Carpenter Manson, Bruce Brooks Pfeiffer, Jack Quinan, Arlene Sanderson, John Sergeant, and posthumously to Henry-Russell Hitchcock and Edgar Kaufmann, Jr. Meg Klinkow of the Frank Lloyd Wright Home and Studio Foundation Research Center, John Geiger and Louis Weihle of the Taliesin Apprentices Association, and Oscar Munoz at the Taliesin Archives also provided valuable information.

For special help with photographs, thanks are due to Melanie Birk and the Frank Lloyd Wright Home and Studio Foundation, John Howe, Joan Lupton and Steelcase, Tony Puttnam, Mildred and Alvin Rosenbaum, and Hollis Weishar and Taliesin Architects.

Finally, I am genuinely appreciative of the Frank Lloyd Wright Building Conservancy and my family for giving me the time to write this book.

Carla Lind

ABOUT THE AUTHOR

Carla Lind has worked for two decades to preserve the legacy of Frank Lloyd Wright. Before being named executive director of the Frank Lloyd Wright Building Conservancy, she served as restoration director for Wright's May house in Grand Rapids, Michigan; this project for Steelcase Inc. won numerous awards including the President's Award honoring the best privately funded restoration and an Honor Award from the American Institute of Architects. Lind previously was executive director of the Frank Lloyd Wright Home and Studio Foundation in Oak Park, Illinois, which administers Wright's first home. She also has lectured on Wright buildings in more than forty cities in the United States and Canada and has served as a preservation consultant to Domino's Pizza for its Frank Lloyd Wright collection as well as to the Wisconsin Governor's Commission on Taliesin. Lind is a graduate of the University of Minnesota, majoring in interior design with an emphasis on the history of architecture. She and her family live near Wright's home in Oak Park, but migrate regularly to their restored farm near his Taliesin in Wisconsin.

The text for *The Wright Style* was composed in Gill Sans, a typeface designed by Eric Gill in 1928 for the Monotype Corporation in England. Gill Sans was modeled after the London Transport type that Edward Johnston designed for the London Underground Railway in 1916. With its clear geometric construction, Johnston's type was much more legible than earlier sans-serif forms.

The display typeface was created especially for *The Wright Style* by Robert L. Wiser of Archetype Press. Named Prairie, this design is based on hand lettering that appears throughout the early drawings of Frank Lloyd Wright, especially during the period in which he was creating his signature Prairie Style houses.